PLEASURE BOATING

IN THE

VICTORIAN ERA

Fig. 2. The *Water Lily* on the Danube. A previously unpublished drawing by Alfred Thompson of the Princess of Thürn and Taxis in the *Water Lily* (see page 8).

PLEASURE BOATING
in the
VICTORIAN ERA

an anthology of some of the more enterprising voyages made in
pleasure boats on inland waterways during the nineteenth century

P.A.L.VINE

Phillimore

1983

Published by
PHILLIMORE & CO. LTD.
Shopwyke Hall, Chichester, Sussex

© P. A. L. Vine, 1983

ISBN 0 85033 504 3

Printed and bound in Great Britain by
THE CAMELOT PRESS LTD
Southampton, Hants

To
Robert Louis Stevenson
(1850–1894)
canoeist extraordinary

By the same author

London's Lost Route to the Sea (1965)
London's Lost Route to Basingstoke (1968)
The Royal Military Canal (1972)
Magdala (1973)
Ethiopia (1974)—unpublished due to coup d'état

CONTENTS

LIST OF ILLUSTRATIONS

PREFACE

FOR MANY PEOPLE the charm of boating is, as Kenneth Grahame wrote, 'simply messing about in boats'. For others it is the excitement of exploring 'unknown' streams, rivers and canals. I have sought in this book to provide a background to those men who loved boating and sought adventure on the inland waterways of Britain and Europe in the latter half of the 19th century. Those who wrote about their experiences were men of art rather than science; even so, they form a varied company, rich and poor, young and middle-aged, bachelors and family men. It is interesting to compare their lives with those of the more famous African and Arctic explorers of the day whom in their own way they reflected in miniature.

During the early part of the 19th century various travellers wrote about their journeys on European waterways. Robert Southey told of his experiences on the passenger barges plying the Dutch and Belgian canals in the autumn of 1815. Michael Quin wrote in *A Stream Voyage down the Danube* (1834) of the excitement of passing the Iron Gate at Djerdap. But these excursions were made by public transport; it is with the independent adventurers who voyaged in their own craft that this book is concerned. The type they employed was multifarious, and in this volume relates to pair-oars, four-oars, skiffs, canoes, a Berri barge, a una boat, a yawl, a catamaran, a rubber dinghy and a steam yacht.

Thomas Peacock's account in *Crotchet Castle* (1831) of four pleasure barges (one for the men, one for the ladies, one for the servants and one for the band) cruising up the Thames and through the Thames & Severn Canal suggests that such voyages may have taken place. However, Philip Hamerton's voyage on the Saone with Joseph Pennell in 1886 was unique in being the first account of a commercial barge being adapted for a pleasure cruise. It was not until Temple Thurston wrote about his experience in the *Flower of Gloster* (1911) that the first account of pleasure barge travel in England appeared. Even so, it was another 30 years before the British public acclaimed L. T. C. Rolt's sensitive and delightfully written *Narrow Boat* (1944) which led to the beginning of a new lease of life for both barges and our waterways and the formation of the Inland Waterways Association (1946).

I have excluded expeditions which were primarily scientific like that of Christopher Costigan who attempted the descent of the Jordan in 1835. I have also made little or no mention of sea cruises and of those better known as ocean going yachtsmen; and I have reluctantly, for reasons of space, omitted reference to Americans like Nathaniel Bishop and Willard Glazier who explored the waterways of the New World.

Of the many people who have so kindly assisted me in this interesting task I would particularly like to mention Mr. Arthur Salter of Salter Brothers Ltd. of Oxford, R. J. Turk & Son of Kingston-upon-Thames, Mr. Peter Fenemore of

Blackwell's, Mr. David Vaisey of The Bodleian Library, Leo Bernard, George Cubitt of the Camping Club of Great Britain, Leslie Weller, Tony Wilsmore, Hugh McKnight, and Charles Hadfield; Emily and Hayward Madden for considerable help and advice about travels in small boats in America before 1900. Mr. Edgar Konsberg provided me with many original Hamerton drawings and Mr. Simon Heneage with an unpublished drawing by Alfred Thompson intended for *The Water Lily on the Danube*; Dr. Mark Baldwin gave considerable help with the bibliography, Mr. B. Babington Smith drew my attention to his family connection with Archibald Smith and his india-rubber boat; Gerald and Joan Griffith advised on matters of art; Michael Cardew also helped; Nigel and Caroline Proddow made possible a finer appreciation of the Thames; Dickon and Phyllis-Anne Dutton-Forshaw offered much comfort on the banks of the Arun; Ean, Jennifer, Jessica, and Helen Begg for encouragement, hospitality and participation. Diana Hanks and Maureen Scantlebury helped with the research. Rosalind Vine was responsible for ensuring not only that the manuscript was presentable but that family voyages with Edwina were more enjoyable than the weather experienced on the Arroux, Arun, Dronne, Western Rother and the Canal du Midi.

Prospect House
Barbados

June 1982

BY WAY OF INTRODUCTION

SYDNEY CROSSLEY, former editor of the *Lock to Lock Times*, writing a few months before the end of the 19th century, stated that 'among the many books which treat of aquatics, no one caters for the large class which prefers the "suaviter in modo" to the "fortiter in re"', and that he was not aware of a single book which satisfactorily dealt with the art of pleasure boating.

Crossley was one of the 'old school'. He held boating to be the most aristocratic of sports and socially acceptable because it had not become 'the child of the book-maker nor the pastime of the rowdy', because the boater was a gentleman and the professional rowing man was 'a thing apart from his fellows' so that Crossley considered it was unnecessary 'even to consider the existence of the class' when dealing with boating as a pastime.

Be that as it may there is little doubt that pleasure boating was very much a middle-class recreation in Victorian times. Rowing or the art of oarsmanship has an ancient history but as a modern sport it dates from 1791 when boat races (Doggett's Coat and Badge) were instituted on the Thames and these were followed by the introduction of regattas, described by the papers of the day as 'a novel amusement newly imported from Venice'. In 1829 the first Oxford and Cambridge boat race took place and the advent of the Henley regatta 10 years later led to widespread publicity being given to rowing.

However, those gentlemen who ceased to race took great pleasure in rowing for exercise or leisure and various types of boat began to be built to cater for the differing needs of the sculler and the family excursionist. Indeed, this volume is about those who first explored, on their own or with friends, the waterways of England and abroad. Although the earliest recorded excursions do not occur before 1850, by the 1830s the rowing of a boat for recreation began to be regarded as a common enough pastime, and Charles Dickens is writing that at Searle's yard at Lambeth on a fine Sunday morning some dozen boats would be ready for the Richmond tide.[1]

Nevertheless, few had the time, money or inclination to go further afield and there is little evidence that there was much pleasure boating above Teddington until the railways brought increasing numbers of day tourists to the upper reaches. It was not, therefore, until the 1850s that boating began to be more generally recognised as a leisure pursuit, a fact recognised by Searle's the boat builders who published the first *Oarsman's Guide to the Thames*.

The Thames has always been the nursery of pleasure boating. As early as 1861 Salters of Oxford had 228 craft for hire which included 12 sculling boats, 12 skiffs,

36 outrigged gigs, 20 dinghies, 15 canoes, 20 punts and 24 funnies (a lightweight pleasure boat whose fore and aft endings were the same). Even so it was the last decades of the century that saw the golden age of boating on the Thames and its tributaries. On the little Wey Navigation pleasure boat tolls rose 12-fold between 1870 and 1893.[2]

While the upper portions of the Thames with a light boat and fine weather were fine for many, the enjoyment of others was better fulfilled by roaming through distant countries with some element of danger and difficulty to be overcome. However, the actual source of enjoyment took different forms.

Mansfield remarked that human nature delighted in doing, seeing and being what fellows had not done, seen or been before and urged his readers to enjoy the pleasure of investigating 'the watery nooks and corners of old Europe'. Above all, noted Mansfield, 'it is the feeling of perfect independence and freedom in those extensive solitudes, where a human being scarcely ever sets his foot and where the silence was only broken by the dull roaring of a rapid, the booming of the bittern or the rattle and rush of the wings of the wild geese' which made their expeditions so enjoyable 'Instead of being the slaves of the time-table of a railway company, here we are starting, stopping, lounging, hurrying just as circumstances or our own fancies dictate'.[3]

MacGregor's purpose was to describe a new mode of travelling on the continent 'by which few people and things are met with, while healthy exercise is enjoyed and an interest ever varied with excitement keeps fully alert the energies of the mind'.[4]

Philip Hamerton sought the assurance of 'finding much that is worth finding and of enjoying many of the sensations which give interest to more famous explorations'.[5]

Warington Baden-Powell preferred 'A stiff breeze, wild scenery, freedom of dress and action, and the perplexities of a strange language, to being guided by a tourist's handbook from a first-class Swiss railway carriage to the comfortable monster hotel with its obsequious English-speaking waiters'.[6]

This sentiment continued to be echoed through the years. In 1878 James Powell writes of the joys of the Weser and its lovely scenery 'without hearing the dreaded names of Cook and Gaze'.

James Molloy pointed out to those who might think small rivers and canals monotonous compared to the Seine or Loire that it was the very tranquility of the little streams and their unknown villages which made a pleasing change from the rush of the great rivers and their big cities.

Such was the philosophy of the Victorians, whose urge to promote rowing was engendered by the belief that this form of exercise was 'good for body and soul, and promotes sound and practical philosophy, in improving health and bodily vigour, and in sweetening the blood and tempers of men'.[6]

Chapter I

LIEUTENANT HALKETT AND THE BOAT-CLOAK (1844)

Invention of the rubber dinghy (1843)—experimental voyage from Kew to Westminster Bridge (1844)—further trips—Franklin Expedition (1845)—explanatory booklet published (1848)—the Knapsack boat awarded prize medal by Commissioners of the International Exhibition (1862).

ONE OF the earliest surviving accounts of a pleasure boat excursion in England was written by Peter Halkett, a lieutenant in the Royal Navy, who on 10 June 1844 made the first recorded trip in a rubber dinghy from Kew to Westminster Bridge with two companions. Halkett had invented the first inflatable boat in 1843 by using india-rubber cloth instead of sealskin to make a boat similar to that used by the Greenland Esquimaux. It was called a boat-cloak or cloak-boat because it could be worn as a cloak until it needed to be converted into a boat. This large-sized mackintosh was provided with an air cylinder which was quickly inflated by bellows. The total weight of cloak, bellows and a pair of paddles was about twelve pounds and its length six feet.

The manuscript log of his 'Good Ship Boat-Cloak' shows the inventor to have had a pleasant sense of humour. It began: 'At sea 10th June 1844 2 o'clock P.M. Lat 51.31 N.Long 2.1W–Chelsea bunhouse bearing North East, by East, half East. — weather cloudy—wind squally—baffling breezes—cross currents—progress retarded— prog. much diminished—grog almost expended—ship's company in low spirits. Shipped a heavy sea of Battersea near Chelsea—Boat Cloak almost on her beam ends —all hands at the pumps—hard work to right her—symptoms of mutiny on board'— Two of the crew ask to go ashore near a Red House on the Battersea coast that they might settle their quarrel like gentlemen—'Captain claps both gentlemen in irons'.

By 3 o'clock the cloud is clearing up and they pass Chelsea. 'Observed on the shore a large Dutch looking round-stern'd building—don't know what to make of it. Not marked on any of our sea charts—Old Tom (our weatherbeaten boatswain) however looked hard at it through his spy-glass, when suddenly squirting the quid out of his mouth, he exclaimed to his messmate 'D--n my eyes Jack if that there big round house bain't the Great Prison they call the Millbank Penny-charity'.'

Passing Lambeth they hoisted their flag and fired salute for Archbishop but salute not returned. At four o'clock the House of Commons was passed to leeward. 'A first rate looking building newly erected on the shore'. Westminster Bridge is reached and the voyage safely concluded.

Halkett made further experimental voyages at various places round the South coast—at Brighton, Portsmouth, Spithead and Plymouth—in the Firth of Tay, the Cove of Cork, the Bay of Dublin, and lastly, in the Bay of Biscay where, in November

1844, he had the opportunity given him of paddling under the critical eyes of a squadron of men-of-war. Upon that occasion his cloak was tried both with its paddle and its umbrella sail, when he managed, in spite of a heavy swell, to pass from HMS *Caledonia* to HMS *St Vincent*—a rather tough trip for although the squadron was lying hove-to, the ships were in fact gradually forging ahead.

3. Lieutenant Halkett's Boat Cloak, 1844

Admiral Sir David Milne, the Commander-in-Chief, Plymouth, offered to forward details of the cloak to the Admiralty and there may well still be a memorandum in the Public Record Office dated 21 January 1845 describing the uses to which the cloth boat might be used to advantage: 'geological surveys, exploring parties, expeditions of discovery' and so on. It was also thought that a larger type might make a suitable ship's lifeboat.

The Admiralty promptly took notice of this note and commanded rubber boats to be made and tested at Portsmouth and Spithead. The Secretary of the Admiralty, however, reported to Halkett on 8 May 1845 that 'My Lords are of the opinion that your invention is extremely clever and ingenious, and that it might be useful in exploring and surveying expeditions, but they do not consider that it could be made applicable for general purposes in the naval service'. Indeed, Captain Sir John Franklin, R.N., who took a rubber boat out with him on his last ill-fated Arctic Expedition (1845) stated that if he had had one with him on his first journey to the Polar Sea (1819–21) it would have enabled the explorers not only to have avoided much of the severe distress which they encountered, when detained for many days on the banks of the Copper Mine River without any means of crossing it, but of probably saving the lives of those who died of famine and fatigue.

Sir George Simpson, of the Hudson Bay Company, took with him a double air boat (intended for Franklin) for the use of the Arctic Land Expedition of 1846–7 since 'I think it', wrote Sir John to a friend in March 1845, 'of such importance to the Land Arctic Expedition which the Hudson's Bay Company are to equip, to be provided with the Cloth-boat, that I willingly resign mine for that service, and will take my chance of having another prepared for me'.

4. The Boat Cloak under sail, 1844

Mr Rae, the leader of that expedition, reported that the rubber boat proved most useful in crossing the river at Repulse Bay and that the fishermen preferred it to their canvas boat when setting nets. The rubber boat carried two men with some two cwt. of stores and was used for six weeks on a rocky coast without needing repair.

Rubber boats began to be manufactured under Halkett's direction by Samuel Matthews of Charing Cross, a firm originally founded by Charles Mackintosh. In 1862 Halkett was awarded a prize medal by the Commissioners of the International Exhibition for his eight-foot-long rubber knapsack boat which could carry two people.

The earliest reference traced of rubber boats being used for pleasure is John MacGregor's diary entry on 22 May 1848 when he 'met Archibald Smith* and saw his india-rubber boat which forms a cloak, tent, boat and bed—perhaps I shall go to the lakes next year'.

* Archibald Smith (1813–1898) was a mathematician and Fellow of the Royal Society. He wrote on the deviation of the compass and like MacGregor was a former member of Trinity College Cambridge. His widow recorded that 'he was a good mechanic, great finish in neatness of work, also ingenuity, great capacity for taking pains'.

5. Contemporary advertisement for the Cloak-Boat

6. Contemporary advertisement for the Knapsack-Boat which won Lieutenant Halkett a prize
medal in the international Exhibition of 1862

Chapter II

ROBERT MANSFIELD AND THE *WATER LILY* (1851–3)

First English rowboat to be taken to the Continent—Robert Mansfield—his athletic prowess —forms a crew—The Log of the Water Lily—chief incidents—publication in book form— sequel The Water Lily on the Danube—Wurzburg to Budapest via King Ludwig's canal and Vienna—third voyage on the Saone and the Rhone (1853)—various editions—Mansfield's later life.

ROBERT MANSFIELD (1824–1908) claimed that he was the first to take an English rowing boat on an excursion to the Continent.* The *Water Lily* was a four-oared Thames gig, 36 feet long, built by Noulton & Wyld of Lambeth. She was adorned with the British Lion painted on her oars and rudder and the Union Jack waving from a brass flagstaff affixed to her bows.

Mansfield was then 27 years of age. He was the son of a Hampshire rector and had spent five years at Winchester where, according to the *Dictionary of National Biography*, 'he never rose above the status of a fag'. After graduating at University College, Oxford he qualified as a barrister, but never practised seriously and long lived a roving life in Scotland and on the Continent. He was a keen shot and one of the first Englishmen to take up golf, which he learnt at Pau in 1857, but his fame rests on his prowess as an oarsman. In 1842–3 he helped to raise his college eight to the head of the river. However, he missed his blue in 1843 when Oxford beat Cambridge with seven oars at Henley and the following year he broke down when in training.

The idea of the expedition was expounded by Mansfield one fine summer's evening in 1851 to a group of barristers congregated in chambers at Pear Tree Court, whose windows overlooked the Thames. His plan, to take a four-oar across the Channel and spend the long vacation exploring the German rivers, was initially greeted with some derision by his colleagues, but in spite of their forebodings, a crew of four oarsmen and a cox was with some difficulty mustered.

The log of the first voyage is of rather limited incident, although on several occasions serious mishaps were only narrowly avoided. At Königswinter, for example, they experienced some excitement when they got entangled among the chains of the flying bridge.

Various stores were procured, but their luggage was not considerable—to 'razors, black hats and gloves we had bid farewell at London'—five leather carpet bags being easily stowed, while portmanteaux were sent on by steamer to the principal towns.

---

* The qualifying word is 'excursion'. Doubtless these were earlier expeditions of a sort. Mansfield quotes the captain of a Moselle steamer saying in 1851 that 'a party of Englishmen some years ago had brought a boat to Coblenz and stopped some time'. Edmund Harvey, the author of *The Cruise of the Undine* mentions (p. 137) that in 1849 he imported a mahogany outrigger pair-oar into Belgium for use while spending two months in Bruges.

The *Water Lily* was hoisted on to the deck of the steamer *Fyrlood* at St Catherine's Wharf in a torrent of rain and shipped to Rotterdam; from there she was transferred to the *Niderlander* which steamed with her up the Rhine for three days. On 31 July 1851 the *Water Lily* was launched at Mannheim. Great was the astonishment of the Mannheimers at seeing five Englishmen clad in grey flannel trousers, white shirts and white felt hats with broad brims 'inserting themselves into an elongated walnut shell'.

From Mannheim they rowed down the Rhine to Cologne, diverging here and there to explore, or have the boat shipped up various tributaries. The crew succeeded in rowing up the Neckar to Heidelberg, but here the torrential stream of the river in flood forced them to return, as even the steamer could not pass under the bridge. Back at their hotel in Mannheim they found the chef up to his knees in water, and at Worms they pulled through the gates into the courtyard and entered the flooded

7. The crew of the *Water Lily* arrive at their flooded hotel at Worms, 1852

hotel through a window, while the ostler put their boat in the stable. In between ascending the Ems, rowing down the Moselle and various sightseeing expeditions, a certain amount of serious rowing was done, including the ascent of the Saar to Saarburg. However, their attempts to row up the Saal from Germünden and the Nabe from Bingen were halted by shallows and rapids.

At Wertheim the Princess of Wertheim and Lowenstein with a party of ladies came to inspect their craft. The crew also met Christiana, a very pretty German girl who joined them with some friends for a picnic *al fresco*, suffered a little by having a soft boiled egg mess up her new polka but who sang to the group quite charmingly before being rowed down in the cool of the evening to Miltenberg.

8. A picnic lunch at Wertheim, 1852

At Berncastel, Mansfield was laid up with gastric fever for a fortnight at the *Three Kings*. He was well nursed by Madame Gassen the landlady, and his cousin also stayed behind. They rejoined the others at Andernach on the Rhine and rowed down to Cologne. The *Water Lily* was sent back via Rotterdam to England and was purchased by a Cambridge friend, A. A. Vansittart of Bisham Abbey.

The first voyage having proved a success, Mansfield planned the following year to descend the Danube to Budapest in a pair-oared boat also named the *Water Lily*. The crew for this trip was his cousin Campbell and undergraduate Alfred Thompson of Trinity College, Cambridge as cox; their rowing dress—large white widewakes, flannel shirts and trousers.

This cruise proved more interesting. The *Water Lily* was shipped to Wurzburg, whence they rowed up the Main and Regnitz to Bamberg which took three days. Beyond Schweinfurt they observed the railway being built alongside the river. 'Crowds of navvies, as many female as male, were busily at work, i.e., they were so till we hove in sight, and then every mattock and spade was dropped, and they remained staring with eyes and mouths open till we were round the next corner out of sight, which, the reaches being long and the stream stiffish, was generally a considerable time. I am afraid that the railway company must have suffered considerably by our transit; and should any crew ever follow in our track, and be prevented, as we were, from going up in the steamer, it would decidedly be to the interest of the company to forward them to Bamberg free of expense'.[7]

At Bamberg they entered King Ludwig's canal which connected the rivers Regnitz and Altmuhl, and formed the 19th-century link between the North Sea and the Black Sea. They were received at the entrance on Friday 30 July with much excitement by the superintendent of the works who, after reading the papers, told them that he had been daily expecting them for a year. The party spent a leisurely eight days covering the 150 miles from Bamberg to Dietfurt which involved passing some hundred locks. Mansfield noted that the canal's lack of commercial success appeared to be due to 'the shallows and rapid stream of the Main Navigation, the lack of water along the canal's summit level and the similarity of the productions at either end'. Consequently they were told it barely paid the working expenses and they saw but few barges on it; however, it had a 'most efficient and numerous staff of officers'. Their printed pass which had to be endorsed at each lock cost five shillings.

'Pulling along the canal was delightfully lazy work after our hundred mile tug up the Main.' From the canal's embankment the scenery was very pretty and alongside ran the river Regnitz, the high road, railway and telegraph. After passing through Forchheim and Nuremberg, they sent the boat on by barge to Feucht to avoid climbing the thirty or so locks. On leaving the *Post Inn* the landlord personally took the trouble to show them a large vaulted apartment which was built on one side of the single-arched aqueduct and carried the canal over a deep gorge shortly before the summit level. After spending the night at Neumarkt on the Sulz where they played skittles, they descended through Beilingries and Berching to Dietfurt where the lock-keeper, who had been one of the Bavarian volunteers under King Otho in Greece, told them the town was 'very bad, inhabited only by old peasants'.

Mansfield noted the curious costumes worn by the ladies: 'gowns very short at the waist, sleeves padded out to an enormous size', admired the Altmuhl valley scenery with its castles perched on the tops of lofty cliffs and delighted in the clarity and rapidity of the river in which they swam. At Kelheim they reached the Danube, and on 9 August rowed down to Ratisbon. At Donaustauf the Princess of Thurn and Taxis invited them to leave their boat at the bathing place and to dine at the chateau. They in turn invited the princess to come for a row, little thinking she would accept, but to their surprise she did; as the stream was very strong and the princess's weight (estimates varied from twelve to fourteen stone) brought down the stern to within two inches of the water, Mansfield was relieved when she was safely landed. Thompson presented the princess with a sketch of the scene of their arrival at the town which Mansfield thought 'most spiritedly executed and will, I am sure, be much prized by its possessor'. (A companion sketch which appears as a frontispiece to this volume was not presumably shown to her!)

The crew ignored the dire warnings about the dangers of attempting to boat down the rocky passage between Wilshofen and Pasau and over the Strudel (rapids) and Wirbel (whirlpools) below Grein. Although white breakers surrounded them on either side, steady pulling and careful steering on both stretches of the river brought the *Water Lily* through without mishap. Indeed, the greatest problems they encountered on the Danube were the shallows between the islands which often obliged them to jump out of the boat to avoid holing her bottom.

9. The *Water Lily* survives the whirlpools of the Wirbel, 1853

After shooting beneath the old stone bridge at Straubing, they spent the night at Deggendorf. The town ominously turned out to a man to see them start but they passed the rapids between Wilshofen and Pasau without mishap and reached Ling. Here they left the boat to make an extensive tour of the region including a seven-hour excursion by train to see the Traun waterfalls at Lambach. They also saw the 420-yard inclined plane which had been built of wood and supported on piers to enable salt barges to pass the fall. Mansfield recorded that 'barges sweep down it at a terrific pace' but does not mention how they returned against the stream. After resuming their train journey to Gemunden they took steamer to Ebensee and carriage and boat to Salzburg, admiring the scenery and visiting a salt mine. Resuming their voyage they lunched on delicious crayfish at a little inn situated at the junction of the Traun and the Danube. At Grein they were greeted by the Singing Club which had composed a song in their honour but by now such adulation by the population had become a bit of a bore. At Dürrenstein they viewed the castle where Richard Coeur-de-Lion had been imprisoned and on arriving at Stein they found that the British colours had been hoisted on a flagstaff in their honour. Near Stein they heard the solemn strains of the chanting of a band of pilgrims. 'It was', said Mansfield, 'a picturesque sight and the sound of the distant melodies floating over the water was very impressive'.

10. The rapids below Linz, 1853

Mooring at the Schanzel by the chain bridge in Vienna, they left the *Water Lily* in the care of 'a friendly bargee' who had witnessed their start from Ratisbon and Linz. Of the many different notices of their proceedings which appeared in no less than nine Viennese papers, all were either misinformed or exaggerated. The only accurate one was sent by the *Morning Chronicle's* foreign correspondent who reported their departure from the Austrian capital some days later. One reason why the papers wrote up their voyage so extensively was the shortage of news due to the very strict press censorship in Vienna—spy fever was rampant and even Thompson's headpiece, 'a sporting wideawake'—was occasion for him to be stopped by a plain clothes police agent, informed that such hats were considered revolutionary and that he must return at once to his hotel to change it. They heard Strauss's band playing, recorded the style of numerous and varied costumes in the streets in some detail and departed Vienna on 31 August 'amid the cheers of the concourse of spectators'.

Beyond Presburg numerous islands and long fleets of floating water mills across the stream and along the banks added to the intricacies of the course. 'Now down a rapid, now grinding on a bank, now wading in the water, now dodging about a number of little islands about an acre in extent' till they reached Gonyo. Caught in a tremendous thunderstorm they clambered up on to a passing barge and sheltered with the crew in the little deckhouse. Below the island of St Andra a magnificent stretch of the Danube led straight to Budapest. 'There were several small islands covered with fine timber trees, and as we passed along, large flocks of wild geese rose into the air, wheeled about for a short time, and then settled down again. Several steamers passing up and down, and long lines of water-mills and barges, proclaimed our near approach to Pesth.'

11. The *Water Lily* reaches Budapest, 1853

The distance from Kitzingen to Budapest was some seven hundred miles and on average they had rowed 28 miles a day on the 25 days they were on the water. The voyage completed, the *Water Lily* was sold to the director of the Danube steamboat company for £12.

Although the narrative suffers from verbose digressions about places visited—churches, salt mines, waterfalls, etc., funny anecdotes, gossip and comment on the idiosyncrasies of foreigners whose habits amused Mansfield and were of perhaps more interest to his contemporaries than they are today, the *Water Lily* on the Danube proved the most entertaining of his voyages.

The log of the *Water Lily* was originally written in a very compressed form for a magazine but never published. It was then hastily issued anonymously (by an Oxford man and a Wykehamist) as a pamphlet (63 pages) in 1852 to advise readers how they might see 'the finest scenery in Europe in an economical novel and delightful manner'. It was then rewritten in rather longer form and published by John

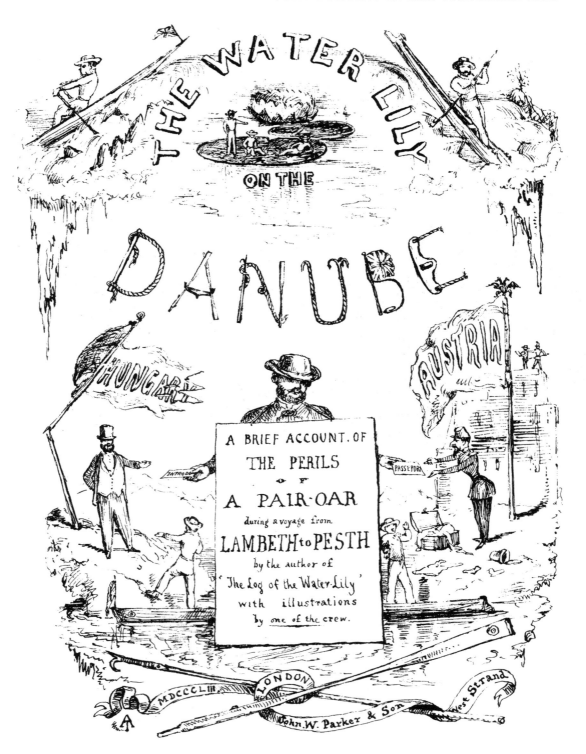

12. Title page drawn by Alfred Thompson for the first edition of
The Water Lily on the Danube, 1853

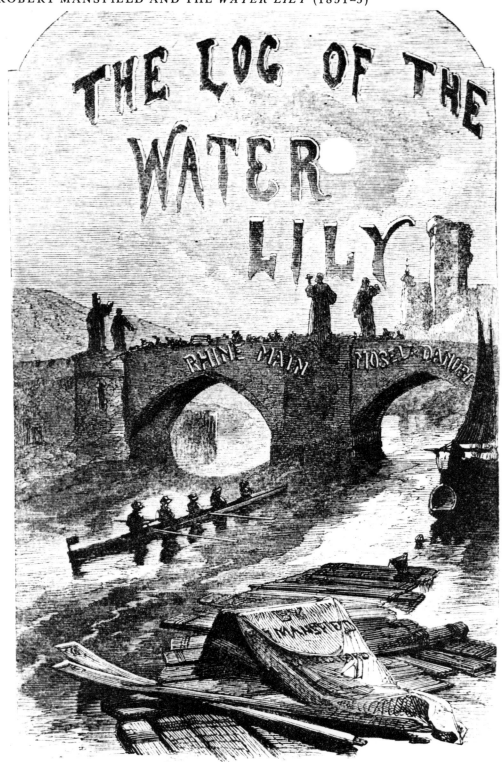

13. Title page of the third edition of *The Log of the Water Lily*, 1854

Parker of the Strand. A sequel *The Water Lily on the Danube* with illustrations by the coxswain, Arthur Thompson, was published in 1853. The two accounts were republished in one volume in 1854, one by W. S. Orr with the illustrations and the other by Nathaniel Cooke without the illustrations, and a fifth edition by Camden Hotten with illustrations appeared 20 years later to which an account of a third and rather uneventful voyage of the *Water Lily* was included. Tauchnitz of Leipzig also included it in their collection of English authors for circulation on the Continent and Routledge also published a sixth English edition when they acquired the copyright.

Mansfield's third cruise was through France in August 1853 in another pair-oar built by Noulton & Wyld. Accompanied by Campbell and A. A. Vansittart, the voyage began on the Burgundy Canal at Dijon. From St Jean de Losne they rowed down the Saone to Lyons and down the Rhône to Beaucaire. Here the *Water Lily* was transferred to a barge and sent by canal to Toulouse while they explored the Pyrenees on horseback. However, Mansfield on reaching Toulouse received a letter demanding his immediate departure for home so that within a quarter of an hour of his arrival he was speeding away in a malle poste drawn by five horses to catch the Bordeaux train to Paris and thence to London. His two companions decided to abandon the remainder of the voyage and sold the *Water Lily*.

The identities of Mansfield's companions on these expeditions was not generally known until the publication of his autobiography *New and Old Chips from an Old*

School Life at Winchester College; or, the Remi-
niscences of a Winchester Junior. By the Author of " The Log of the Water Lily," and " The Water Lily on the Danube." Second edition, revised, coloured plates, 7s. 6d.   [*In preparation.*

⁂ This book does for Winchester what " Tom Brown's School Days" did for Rugby.

Log of the " Water Lily" (Thames Gig), during Two
Cruises in the Summers of 1851-52, on the Rhine, Neckar, Main, Moselle, Danube, and other Streams of Germany. By R. B. MANS-FIELD, B.A., of University College, Oxford, and illustrated by ALFRED THOMPSON, B.A., of Trinity College, Cambridge.   [*In preparation.*

⁂ This was the earliest boat excursion of the kind ever made on the Continental rivers. Very recently the subject has been revived again in the exploits of Mr. MacGregor in his " Rob Roy Canoe." The volume will be found most interesting to those who propose taking a similar trip, whether on the Continent or elsewhere.

---

14. Advertisement for Mansfield's books, 1853

Block in 1896. In this he revealed that the crew on the first voyage consisted of F. Bernard (cox), the former cox of the Oriel Torpid; Sir Henry Halford (stroke), a well-known rifle shot; G. Slater Booth (later Lord Basing) no. 3; Mansfield (no. 2) and his cousin a Cambridge graduate John Campbell (bow) who became inspector of factories. All the rest were Oxford men. Booth's place at Coblenz was taken by Fellowes (later attorney-general in Melbourne).

Mansfield married Colonel L'Estrange's daughter Sophie at the British Embassy in Brussels in 1858 by whom he had two daughters. He wrote various works, including *School Life at Winchester College* (1866), and edited the treatise by his brother Charles on *Aerial Navigation* (1877) and *Letters from the Camp before Sebastopol* by a cousin, Colonel C. F. Campbell (1894). Late in life he settled in London and became a member of the vestry and guardian for St George's, Hanover Square. He died in 1908.

Chapter III

EDMUND HARVEY'S CRUISE IN THE *UNDINE* (1853)

Edmund Harvey—author and musical composer—pair-oar expedition through France, Baden, Rhenish Bavaria, Prussia, and Belgium—a pleasing and well written story—published anonymously (1854).

EDMUND HARVEY (1828–1884) was a Cornishman who took holy orders in 1854 and who succeeded his father as rector of Truro in 1860 and became vicar of Mullion in 1865. He was much interested in churches, church music and wrote numerous ecclesiastical and musical works; also a history of Mullion in 1875. As a boy he enjoyed walking and went on a tour of Northamptonshire with his brother in 1846. After graduating at Queen's College, Cambridge, where he was captain of the boat club, he resided for several years on the Continent. However, it was from London that he and two colleagues decided in 1853 to make a pair-oar expedition across Europe. It was the year before his ordination and Harvey, who published his account anonymously, stated in his preface that one reason for his narrative was that although he had not had the good fortune to come across the *Log of the Water Lily* he had enjoyed perusing the *Water Lily on the Danube*. He admitted that having spent some time on the rivers and canals in Cambridgeshire, he had often wished to be party to a more extensive voyage. And so when the 'Professor' suggested a continental cruise in a pair-oar, the matter was settled.

The trio met in London in June to plan their six-week trip and adopt 'noms de voyage'—Harvey as captain, while the other two were known as the 'Doctor' and the 'Professor'. Noulton & Wyld of Lambeth provided a similar pair-oar to Mansfield's second *Water Lily*. The crew each equipped themselves with 'an alpaca coat for town, light waistcoat ditto, two shirts, two merino jerseys, one sky blue flannel ditto, two pairs of flannel trousers, two pairs of socks, four pocket handkerchiefs, a pair of canvas shoes, a comb and toothbrush and a mackintosh'.

After travelling by boat and train from Newhaven to Paris, they hired a cart and, accompanied by a Mr Arthur who was the founder and secretary of the Paris Boat Club,* they set off to launch the *Undine* at Asnieres. Here a couple of days were spent meeting and being entertained by club members as well as rowing to St Cloud and back before the *Undine* left Paris. They spent an uncomfortable first night at an auberge on the Seine near Juvisy. The landlady refused to admit them until they had changed out of their boating costume. The inn was full of rowdy bargees and the beds so damp that they had to lie on their mackintoshes. After rowing against the current past Corbeil and Meulan to Montereau, they followed the Yonne to Sens and Laroche where they entered the Burgundy Canal. Here they observed that horses

---

* It consisted then of about 20 members with six or seven boats. Lord Cowley was president.

were seldom used to tow the barges. Instead, mother on one bank, son on the other, hauled while father steered. Some of the lock-keepers fancied they were canal inspectors which caused them to take a lively interest in the state of the locks and the account books submitted for their inspection. This may have been because the Emperor was due to pass along the canal in a few days' time and they were mistaken for the officials to pilot his steamer.

At Dijon they observed three desecrated churches being used as a vegetable market, a corn exchange and a stable for the cavalry. They called on M. Baumgarten the engineer of the Canal du Rhon au Rhin for advice and at St Jean de Losne were

15. The crew of the *Undine* arrive at St Jean de Losne, 1853

greeted with intense curiosity by the local people who treated them with great civility and respect. People began to collect from three in the morning to see them start and they left the town 'amidst tumultuous cheering and great waving of hand-kerchiefs'. From the Saone they passed on to the Canal du Rhon au Rhin.

At Rochefort on the Doubs the crew had to share a bedroom at the village inn with three bargees. The following night they shared the only room at a roadside inn with nine other people. Indeed, they rarely spent a comfortable night. At Gernsheim they stayed at a small house by the riverside, where the mosquitoes forced them to wear their mackintoshes in bed and smoke their pipes. Morning found them bleary-eyed, their hands and faces covered with blotches and bites.

A minor mishap a few miles past the junction of the Basle & Strasburg Canal nearly brought the excursion to a halt. Because of the noon-day heat, the *Undine* was being hauled from the towpath when they met an empty fly barge drawn by two horses. The *Undine*'s bow-line became entangled with that of the barge and before it could be cut, the stern of the barge had scraped the pair-oar, breaking two of her thwarts. A carpenter at Kembs was found to make a new set of elbows and 24 hours later all had been repaired. There then arose a problem over the account. Robert, the carpenter, wanted 15 francs, his companion four, while the Professor offered five in all. The dispute was referred to the village mayor, a plain rustic in sabots, who finished feeding his pigs, washed his hands and sat in judgment. After an hour's palaver, an award of six francs fifty centimes was made to the workmen so, except for the loss of time, the crew was well satisfied with the outcome.

The stretch of the Rhine between Huningen and Strasburg was in flood with a tremendous flow and this proved the most hazardous part of their trip. The navigation of the river, 'cut up by innumerable islands and sandbanks necessarily abounds in rapids and falls in water', required considerable skill as well as caution. They nearly capsized several times when the swift current caught the keel of the boat, making it impossible to steer her. At times they estimated they were racing along at fifteen to eighteen miles an hour. Once the boat's stern swung round over the edge of a whirlpool and, should the boat have capsized, the fate of the Doctor, who could not swim, might well have been sealed. 'Now we are sweeping down a rapid

16. Avoiding a whirlpool on the Upper Rhine below Alt Breysach, 1853

so shallow that we can see the bottom, and rush past the trunk of an old tree, which itself seems as if it was being pulled up against the stream by some invisible power; now we reach the end of the *shallow*, and the water is boiling and bubbling about us in all directions, and the sharp crested waves come rattling against the side of the boat like so many undertakers at work.'[8]

17. Passing shallows on the Upper Rhine, 1853

The 70 miles from Neumburg to Kehl was covered in six hours and a quarter and the Doctor doubted if even the *Water Lily* on the Danube had met with such a continuous rapid stream.

At Mannheim the *Undine* was stowed in the same stable used by the *Water Lily*. The crew found the row against the stream of the Neckar to Heidelberg extremely arduous and, where there were rocks, the crew had to jump out and wade. At Heidelberg they joined old friends, went sight-seeing and witnessed a duel between two students which took place in the house of a fisherman.

The voyage down to Cologne proved uneventful and rather than continue down the Rhine to Rotterdam, they placed the *Undine* in a railway truck full of wool sacks and sent her to Ghent, whence they rowed to Bruges where the Professor

18. Shooting the Bridge of Boats at Cologne, 1853

departed for home. Harvey and the Doctor rowed on to Ostend and then returned to Bruges where Harvey built himself an outrigger funny or wager boat. This accomplishment was well written up in the Bruges newspaper, *L'Impartial*, which termed 'the owner' an 'intrepide et indefatigable canotier', so that it was not long before he was addressed in public as Monsieur le Chef des Regates.

Harvey's account is pleasing and well presented. It has more local colour and fewer digressions than Mansfield's work but both authors suffered from a lack of moving experience whether mental or physical. There is little dialogue or characterisation and the reader learns little more about the author and his two companions than their trivial delights and aggravations. However Harvey, too, reiterated Mansfield's joy of independent travel and added 'we all had an objection to doing a town in the customary manner of Englishmen abroad—that of seeing the greatest number of things in the least possible time'.

Our Cruise in the Undine was issued anonymously in 1854 by John Parker, the same publishers as the *Log of the Water Lily*. It contained a set of delightful etchings by one of the crew as well as pictorial initial chapter lettering. It did not achieve the same degree of literary success as Mansfield and has not been reprinted.

Chapter IV

JOHN MACGREGOR AND HIS VOYAGES IN THE *ROB ROY* (1865-72)

'The Rob Roy, *first (of oak) canoed a trip at ease*
By paddle, sail and cart through forest, lake and seas.'

The growth in popularity of canoeing–John MacGregor–the Rob Roy *canoe–account of his voyage through Europe in 1865–publication of* A Thousand Miles in the Rob Roy Canoe *(1866)–founding of the Canoe Club (1866)–*Rob Roy *on the Baltic (1866)–the yawl* Rob Roy*–The Voyage Alone across the English Channel to Paris (1867)–expedition to the Near East (1868-9)–MacGregor paddles through the Suez Canal–meets H. M. Stanley–captured by Arabs–publication of* Rob Roy *on the Jordan (1869)–cruises on the Texel (1871) and in the Shetlands (1872)–MacGregor marries and abandons boating–lecture successes–long illness–achievements.*

THE RAPID RISE in the popularity of canoeing was largely due to John MacGregor (1825-1892), who designed his own Rob Roy canoes and described his voyages in a series of narratives which won wide public acclaim. MacGregor was a man of many parts for, besides being a philanthropist, traveller and barrister-at-law, he was a good organiser, lecturer and publicist. He was the son of General Sir Duncan MacGregor and when he was but five weeks old he survived the loss of the *Kent*, an East India-man which caught fire in the Bay of Biscay. His love of boating dated from boyhood when he was allowed to manage a boat on the Grand Junction Canal at Weedon in Northamptonshire. Later, at the age of 15, he was fortunate not to have drowned when his iron sailing cutter sank in a heavy sea outside Kingstown Harbour.

After leaving school, MacGregor went to Trinity College Dublin and then to Trinity College, Cambridge, where he was a popular boating man although he failed to keep his place in the first eight. He was called to the Bar at the Inner Temple in 1851 and applied himself to patent law. However, having adequate private means, he preferred to devote himself to propagating the Gospel, supporting the London Scottish Rifle Volunteers, foreign travel and active philanthropic pursuits such as the Shoeblack Society. He was in Paris during the revolution of 1848 and the following year made his first long journey in the Middle East. At Malta he 'dined with the Governor and sailed in his yacht', visiting the island on which St Paul was shipwrecked and then swimming 'to the mainland taking the same course which St Paul and his company must have escaped by. Read the account of the wreck in the Acts'.[9]

In 1853 MacGregor ascended Mont Blanc and Vesuvius, and after visiting America, went to Russia in 1859. In 1861 he voyaged down the Danube 'in a splendid steamer', travelled on to Greece and then to North Africa. It was not until 1865 that he started on the first of his famous canoe voyages. He relates that his interest in canoeing was aroused in May 1848 by seeing Archibald Smith's india-rubber boat (see Chapter I) and bed.[10] However, it was another 17 years before MacGregor started on the first of those solitary cruises by which he became so well known.

19. John MacGregor (1825–1892), traveller, philanthropist, creator of the Rob Roy canoe and founder of the Royal Canoe Club

The first Rob Roy canoe was built of oak by Searle's of Lambeth and covered fore and aft with cedar. She was made short enough to go into a German railway waggon, measuring 15 feet in length, 28 inches in breadth, and nine inches in depth. Her weight was 80 pounds and she drew three inches of water. Besides a twin-bladed paddle seven feet long, she had a mast, lug sail and jib; a silk Union Jack fluttered at the prow and the name *Rob Roy* was painted in blue letters on the stern.[11]

The first European voyage MacGregor planned led over mountains, through forests, across plains and involved navigating no less than 11 rivers, including the Rhine, the Danube, the Reuss, and the Marne, venturing upon six lakes and touching upon six canals in Belgium and France. Being a fair draughtsman, MacGregor, sketch-book in boat, illustrated his exploits.

MacGregor's dress consisted of a grey flannel suit and a Norfolk jacket with shoulder straps, six pockets and belted at the waist which survived his first four voyages without a button damaged. A Cambridge straw hat, canvas wading shoes, blue spectacles and a spare suit for Sunday and evening wear completed his wardrobe.

The *Rob Roy* left Westminster Bridge on top of the tide on 29 July 1865 in hot weather. The cruise to Southend was followed by a railway trip along the pier to catch the steamboat to Sheerness from whence the London Chatham & Dover Railway Co. carried the canoe on the coals of the engine tender to Dover. From Ostend the canoe was entrained to Brussels, carried through the city on a cart to another station and unloaded at Namur where it was housed for the night in the landlord's private parlour, resting 'gracefully' upon two chairs. From this point the voyage on the Meuse began.

20. MacGregor races a herd of cattle across the Meuse

At Liege he was joined by the Earl of Aberdeen* who had a canoe made of fir built for the trip. They paddled to the fortified town of Maastricht, took the train to Cologne, the steamer up the Rhine to Bingen and Mainz, and on again by rail to Asschaffenburg, where the canoes sailed down the Main to Frankfurt from whence his 'active and pleasant' companion had to return to England.

MacGregor took the train to Freiburg and thence by cart to the source of the Danube at Donaueschingen from which village he canoed downstream, passing islands of all shapes and sizes; the scenery to Friedingen and Beuron surpassed that of the Wye, with magnificent crags reaching high up on both sides and impenetrable forests. At every town the arrival of his canoe aroused great interest. Leaving Tuttlingen at six in the morning the bridge and its approaches were crowded and one

21. The *Rob Roy* leaves Tuttlingen on the upper reaches of the Danube, 1865. 'A picture can never repeat the shouts and bustle or the sound of guns firing and bells ringing which on more than one occasion celebrated the *Rob Roy's* morning paddle.'

man 'respectfully asked him to delay his start for five minutes as his aged father wished exceedingly just to see the canoe'. At Riedlingen the excitement about the boat 'became almost ridiculous' and at least a thousand people gathered on the bridge and its approaches to see the boat start.[12]

From Ulm he took the train to Frederickshaven on Lake Constance, and after a paddle on the lake our adventurer sought out the Rhine, crossed Lake Zeller, spent the night at the town of Stein and continued to the rapids at Schaffhausen,† from which point he caught the train to Zurich. After cruising upon lakes Zurich, Zug and Lucerne, MacGregor left by the rapid river Reuss. In the more lonely parts 'the trees were in dense thickets to the water's edge, and the wild ducks fluttered out

---

* His father, the fourth earl, had been Prime Minister 1852-5 and his brother, the Hon. James Gordon, a Cambridge rowing blue, was an expert canoeist and the first to cross the English Channel in a Rob Roy.
† The famous falls where Viscount Montague, the owner of Cowdray House at Midhurst, drowned while attempting to boat over them in 1791. On the same day the family mansion was destroyed by fire.

from them with a splash, and some larger birds like bustards often hovered over the canoe'. After Imyl, the river banks assumed a new character. 'They were steep and high and their height increased as we advanced between the two upright walls of stratified gravel and boulders.' The dull heavy roar round the bank of the river grew louder, and it was here that MacGregor had his most exciting moments, for the canoe was swept over a sloping ledge of flat rocks and 'there came in sight the great white ridge of tossing foam where the din was great and a sense of excitement and confusion filled the mind'. Right in front and in the middle he saw the six-foot high wave into which the canoe was impelled by the mighty stream. 'The boat plunged

22. John MacGregor paddling over the rapids of the Reuss, 1865. 'Now and then the stream was so swift that I was afraid of losing my straw hat.'

headlong into the shining mound of water as I clenched my teeth and clutched my paddle. We saw her sharp prow deeply buried, and then before she could rise the mass of solid water struck me a heavy blow full in the breast, closing round my neck as if cold hands gripped me and quite taking away my breath.'[13] The canoe passed on unscathed and MacGregor's coat, while drenched in front, was scarcely wet behind; soon he was at the Roman town of Bremgarten. 'Down by the shady trees, under the towering rocks, over the nimble rapids and lurching among orchards, vineyards and wholesome scented hay', the canoe continued downstream, to where the Reuss was joined by the Limmet and the Aar, before reaching the Rhine at Waldshut in the Grand Duchy of Baden on 12 September.

23. Portage—by cow-cart

Some danger was experienced in going too close to the Lauffenburg falls (above which point a cow was found to draw the cart which carried the canoe to the hotel), and those of Rheinfelden also created some difficulties as well as excitement. 'Imagine some hundreds of acres all of water in white crested waves, varied only by black rocks resisting a struggling torrent, and a loud thundering roar mingled with a strange hissing as the spray from ten thousand sharp-pointed billows is tossed into the air.' The *Rob Roy* survived these knocks and strains without injury, and it was not until later that her planks and timbers were tortured by rough usage.

Between Rheinfelden and Bale, MacGregor regretted returning to civilisation and the loss of that pleasant simplicity which he had hitherto experienced. 'Here we have composite candles and therefore no snuffers.' Here, too, he saw men pulling along a barge and having to walk among the bushes on the bank and often wade in the Rhine itself where there was no towpath. At both Lauffenburg and Bale he learnt more of the exploits of the four-oared boat which with five Englishmen had been sent out overland from London to Schaffhausen for the descent of the Rhine some six weeks before. Since they had passed the rapids in a time of flood when the rocks were covered, they arrived safely in Bale, their clothes and baggage drenched; the writer commented with a malicious grin that 'thereby his friend the washer-woman had earned twenty seven francs in one night'.

At Bale, MacGregor left the Rhine and after a portage found a branch of the semi-derelict Rhône & Rhine canal whose traffic was so little that at best 'it would not pay to buy water for its supply'; a fork of this canal led to Mulhouse, but as the railway authorities refused to carry his canoe, the *Rob Roy* had to continue by the Bale canal where MacGregor found the locks very objectionable, not because he worked them, but because he had to portage each one with the aid of any on-lookers present to whom 'if the man looks poor I give him a few sous'. At some of the locks the lock-keepers asked for his canal pass, but he laughed the matter off and when they pressed it with a 'mais monsieur', he treated the proposal as a good joke until the officials gave in, not because he refused to pay the toll but because he had failed to get a permit at the entrance of the navigation. After spending two nights in an inn at Illfurth, he continued along the canal for a lock or two, but found 'this sort of travelling so insufferable' since it involved going over the hills by a series of tedious locks 'which had already been traversed by the four-oar boat *Waterwitch* some years ago'. There were, however, difficulties to be overcome in finding a cart, and to make matters worse part of the canal had been drained for lock repairs. Finally, a bullock carted the *Rob Roy* to Thann where she was transferred to the newly-opened railroad to Wesserling, whence a comfortable four-wheeled carriage was hired for the 35-mile trek over the watershed of the Vosges mountains to the village of Bussang, where the Moselle was found to be the size of

24. The *Rob Roy* avoiding rocks on the Rhine at Rheinfelden. MacGregor wrote in 1880 that several canoeists had since passed the falls but 'an upset had been the rule'.

a babbling brook. After spending the night at Remire in a 'bad sort of inn where all was disorder and dirt', the canoe was launched a mile away. 'Pretty water flowers quivered in the ripples round the mossy stones . . . The water of this river was very clear and cool, meandering through long deep pools, and then over gurgling shallows; and the fish, water-fowl, woods and lovely green fields were a most welcome change from the canal we had left.'

25. Washerwomen on the Moselle

MacGregor was diverted by the washerwomen on the Moselle, and concluded that the 'respectability' of a town could be measured by the size and ornaments of the blanchisseuses' float. In the smaller villages where there was no barge for their use, the women knelt on the ground and so along all parts of the river they were to be found whacking away, slapping and scrubbing linen while they talked. The water level was the lowest for 30 years due to the drought, and after spending nights at Epinal and Chatel, MacGregor came to the point where the Moselle became so narrow, with vertical rock banks, that he was reminded of 'the rock cutting near Liverpool on the old railway to Manchester'. Further on the stream was contained in a rock channel not five feet wide but three to 20 feet deep, and eventually the canoe had to be dragged some 'hundred yards over most awkward rocks'. Before reaching Charmes he saw lying some 10 feet down the upper part of a fine Ionic column, a white marble pedestal and a broken pediment of large dimension, but how these subaqueous relics had come to be there remained a mystery.

The Moselle had now become less interesting, so from Charmes MacGregor took the train to Blainville on the river Meurthe where he came upon for the first time two French youths rowing for exercise. Then to a great weir 15 feet in height followed by a maze of shallows and much tiresome hauling of the canoe. Consequently, MacGregor had resource to the busy canal to Nancy; thence the canoe went by rail to the river Marne at Epernay. The boat suffered bruising during its journey in the luggage van and emergency repairs had to be made at the first village. Various chains and stone barrages were a hindrance during the 200 or so miles voyage down the Marne. As he canoed through the champagne country he noticed Madame Clicquot's house. After spending the night in the *Elephant Hotel* at Chateau Thierry he observed the rafts, 'some made of casks lashed together with osiers, some made of planks, others of hewn logs and others of great rough trees. The straw hut on each is for the captain's cabin and the crew have to spend up to a fortnight to drag and push them to the Seine'. At Nogent the weather, after six weeks of brilliant sunshine, became cooler; now and then a pleasure boat was seen, and there were several flat-bottomed canoes (périssoires) at some of the towns.

'At Meaux there was a bridge with houses on it and great millwheels filling up the arches as they did in Old London Bridge.' Seeing a canal lock open between Meaux and Lagny he paddled in 'merely for variety' and passed soon into a tunnel (later blown up during the Franco-Prussian War) 'in the middle of which there was a huge boat fixed, and nobody with it. The boat exactly filled the tunnel and the men had gone to their dinner, so I had first to drag their huge boat out, and then the canoe proudly glided into daylight, having a whole tunnel to itself.' Entering another canal to cut off a bend in the river, it presently began to fill with weeds, then clumps of great rushes, then bushes and trees all growing with thick grass in the water and MacGregor had a hard struggle to force his way through this dense marsh. That night he was badly housed in the garret of *The Jolly Rowers* at Neuilly (the canoe stayed in a summer house). Numerous islands made the best channels difficult to find and as he approached Paris the river banks were now dotted with villas and numerous pleasure boats were moored at neat little stairs.

However, the barge traffic on the Marne went straight through a canal cut while the river went off in a wide curve which MacGregor laboriously followed until at length he came to the Seine and the island of Notre Dame. After some difficulty in finding somewhere to berth the *Rob Roy*, he must have appeared an odd sight arriving at the fashionable *Hotel Meurice* with his luggage on his shoulders. MacGregor returned to Charing Cross by train and paddled with a flowing tide on a sunny evening straight to Searle's boat-house. So ended MacGregor's first voyage in the *Rob Roy* — a voyage which was publicised in the British, French, German, and even American press.

MacGregor related that 'the pleasure of meandering with a new river is very peculiar and fascinating. Each few yards brings a novelty, or starts an excitement. A crane jumps up here, a duck flutters there, splash leaps a gleaming trout by your side, the rushing sound of rocks warns you round that corner, or anon you come

26. MacGregor attempting to paddle through an abandoned cut on the Marne

suddenly upon a millrace. All these, in addition to the scenery and the people and
the weather, and the determination that you must get on, over, through, or under
every difficulty, and cannot leave your boat in a desolate wold, and ought to arrive
at a house before dark, and that your luncheon bag is long since empty; all these,
I say, keep the mind awake, which would doze away and snore for 100 miles in a
railway carriage.'[15]

  A Thousand Miles in the Rob Roy Canoe on Twenty Lakes and Rivers of Europe,
with woodcuts from the author's drawings, was published in January 1866. Within
a month a new edition was printed. *The Times* gave the book two and a quarter
columns of unmixed praise and the second edition of 2000 copies was sold out in
five days. The Emperor Napoleon III read it and decreed 'an exhibition of pleasure-
boats' in 1867. MacGregor promptly sent him a specially bound copy and a photo-
graph.[16] In May a third edition came out. By the end of the year 8000 copies had
been sold. (The 11th edition appeared in 1880; the 21st in 1908.)

  MacGregor's popularity lay in his appeal to the adventurous Englishman who
wanted to be a traveller rather than a tourist. A protest even in 1865 to the pack-
aged tour and the ardent followers of Baedeker: 'Year after year it is enough of

excitement to some tourists to be shifted in squads from town to town, according to the routine of an excursion ticket. Those who are a little more advanced will venture to devise a tour from the many pages of Bradshaw, and with portmanteau and bag, and hatbox and sticks, they find more than enough of judgment and tact is needed when they arrive in a night train, and must fix on an omnibus in a strange town. Safe at last in the bedroom of the hotel, they cannot but exclaim with satisfaction: "Well, here we are all right at last!"'

'But after mountains and caves, churches and galleries, ruins and battlefields have been pretty well seen, and after tact and fortitude have been educated by experience, the tourist is ready for new lines of travel which might have given him at first more worry than pleasure, and these he will find in deeper searches among the natural scenery and national character of the very countries he has only skimmed before.'

'The rivers and streams on the Continent are scarcely known to the English tourist, and all the beauty and life upon them no one has well seen.

'In his Guidebook route, indeed, from town to town, the tourist has crossed this and that stream—has admired a few yards of the water, and has then left it for ever. He is carried again on a noble river by night in a steamboat, or is whisked along its banks in a railway, and, between two tunnels, gets a moment's glimpse at the lovely water, and lo! it is gone.

'But a mine of rich beauty remains there to be explored, and fresh gems of life and character are waiting there to be gathered. These are not mapped and labelled and ticketed in any handbook yet and better so, for the enjoyment of such treasures is enhanced to the best traveller by the energy and pluck required to get at them.'[17]

The enthusiasm which greeted the publication of his canoe voyage caused him to found the Canoe Club, 'To improve canoes, promote canoeing and unite canoeists'. The first meeting was held at the *Star and Garter*, Putney, on 27 July 1866, when 20 members were enrolled and MacGregor elected captain. Any gentleman who owned a canoe or hired one by the year could be proposed and elected a member— 'one blackball in five to exclude'. The first list of members included distinguished oarsmen, travellers, alpine climbers and athletes and within a few months the club was patronised by HRH The Prince of Wales, who accepted the invitation to become the first commodore.

The minutes of the first meeting of the Canoe Club announced that voyages were already planned for the summer of 1866 for England, Wales, Scotland, Ireland, Norway, Sweden, Denmark, etc.. Certainly the year saw the *Rattlesnake* launched in the Trent, the *Robin Hood* being paddled to Windermere, the *Rapid* and the *Rover* starting for Scotland while the *Ripple* set off for the Rhine. The *Rambler* was touring 'promiscuously' while it was hoped that the *Reverie, Ranger*, and *Romp* would soon float gaily. Several members, it appeared, were also intending to meet with their canoes and dogs on the Clyde. The logs of club members contained details of many amusing adventures as well as three or four upsets and 'canoe catastrophies', but only a single life lost—that of a dog. One member bumped into a bridge on the Severn and was left clinging to it while his boat departed bottom upwards. Another went over a weir sideways, the occupant upset and the canoe broken to pieces. A third struck on a lasher and was capsized twice in two days while another coming in on a rough sea was seized by a crowd of compassionate fish wives, watching for him on shore, who carried the man and his boat in their brawny arms, rescuing him as though he had protested 'I will be drowned; nobody shall save me'. To all of which reports the *Pall Mall Gazette* commented that the Canoe Club 'unites the maximum of danger and discomfort with the minimum of utility' which caused MacGregor to urge the writer to join their club and recover his good humour.[18]

There were strange if not wholly unexpected reactions from some Victorians. One who had just spent his vacation in Brighton asked MacGregor 'was it not a great waste of time?' and another said: 'Don't you think it would have been more commodious to have had an attendant with you to look after luggage and things?' Membership of the club increased and many voyages took place in 1866. One rowing blue (the Hon. James Gordon) sailed his canoe across the Channel to Boulogne and paddled through France to the Mediterranean (see page 122).

A second paddled across the Channel from France, a third went down the Danube, the Moldau and the Elbe. A fourth carried a dog on board which on shore dragged the canoe on wheels. Three went round the rocky coast of Skye, of whom two crossed to the island of Rum. Others cruised the Clyde, the Thames, the Irish streams, while one took his boat to India and another to Australia.[19]

In 1866 MacGregor took a new and smaller canoe through Scandinavia and described his experiences in *The Rob Roy on the Baltic*. This canoe, again built by Searle, was 'shorter (12 ins.), narrower (2 ins.), shallower (½ in.) and lighter (9 lbs)'. The *Rob Roy* was shipped to Norway and reached Christiania (Oslo) on 2 August. She was then entrained 60 miles to Kongsvinger and then moved by dresine (a carriage on rails moved by cranks and treadles) to the banks of a small lake. From this point MacGregor intended paddling to Stockholm. However, although the map showed a stream leading from this lake to join a series of other lakes, no outlet could be found and he was fortunate to obtain the help of military men on manoeuvres who had it moved to a nearby stretch of water (the Vrangs Elv) that led to another lake. Navigation proved more difficult than expected since some of the lakes had numerous islands, many unmarked on the map, and it was impossible to tell which were which. Consequently, MacGregor had to keep stopping at islands to climb headlands to find the way. Another problem was the logs of timber near the sawmills, and at one point the timber reached along the Vrangs as far as the eye could see. There was nobody in sight, no house, and so MacGregor had first to carry the luggage up through the forest and then drag the *Rob Roy*. Into Sweden, and by a series of lakes and a portage by cart to lake Venern and the town of Karlstadt from which point steamers were taken to and through the West Gotha Canal. 'The steamer's swell rushed along the canal banks, and the tall green reeds bent down in low bows while the waves burst with a splash among the bushes and chased the little sea-sparrows from their night haunts chirping angrily.'

The locks were always opened by women, who worked 'furiously' though it looked odd enough to see young lasses with great crinolines perched high aloft, turning the winch handles. 'As morning went on the country girls came to sell fresh

27. Portage—by railway dresine

raspberries in pretty baskets of birch bark, and butter and woodcocks.' The steamer got its supplies cheaply in this way and so was able to provide passengers with 'a neat bill of fare with very little to pay'.

The West Gotha Canal led into Lake Viken and then into Lake Vettern, where MacGregor stopped at Vadstena to see an old friend. Entering the Motala river he passed through a chain of lakes, a canal or two and many locks including a flight of 11 into lake Roxen en route for Norrköping and the Baltic.

After spending a week in Stockholm, where MacGregor was surprised to find that there were 'scarcely any' pleasure boats to be seen, he took the steamer to Orebro and the train to Töreboda where he had a long sail on the West Gotha Canal. He continued by rail to Gothenburg, by steamer to Lake Venern, and by the Carl's Graf Canal to Trolhetta, whose falls are negotiated by a series of locks to the beautiful river Gota, where two whirlpools were easily passed. Then by steamer back to Gothenburg and on to Copenhagen via Helsingborg.

In Copenhagen the *Rob Roy* attracted a great crowd and the canoe was lodged on an ottoman in the great ballroom of the hotel for the night. Then by train across Zeland and by boat to Svendberg and Sönderburg, where he visited the scene of the battle between the Danes and the Prussians during the Schleswig-Holstein

28. Portage—on foot

war only two years earlier (1864). From Flensburg the *Rob Roy* was mounted on
top of a railway carriage to Hamburg, where MacGregor paddled round the harbour,
along the Elbe to Gluckstadt and then took the steamer to Heligoland, still a British
colony 'and a very curious interesting place'.

'We land from large boats, being carried on men's backs through the last rolling
wave' on to this flat grassy-topped rock with vertical red sides and a cluster of white,
blue and grey houses at its foot. The Governor was both 'a canoe man and a guards-
man' on whose table lay the account of last year's *Rob Roy* voyage, so MacGregor

29. Portage—by horse and cart

was a welcome guest for three days. Returning to Bremerhaven, he made 'a long and delightful trip' up the Weser before sailing back by steamer to the Thames. MacGregor estimated that in two months he had travelled a thousand miles and more by canoe (300 sailing), that 500 miles had been covered by rail, and that 25 steamers had borne him and the *Rob Roy* another thousand over river, lake and sea. His expenses totalled £45.

Immediately upon his return he rewrote the notes of his trip in literary form with the result that in December 1866 there appeared *The Rob Roy on the Baltic*. Another phenomenal success attended the publication of this book and revived the sale of the former one. Already some 200 *Rob Roy* canoes had been built. The papers were full of articles about canoes and canoeing, which aroused much comment and controversy. Some felt coasting trips by canoe 'not worth the candle when you can go by steamer', others that a canoe was only of use for water impracticable for other kinds of boats. Some felt it a duty to protest against the claims of an 'upstart phenomenon to share in the unapproachable merit possessed by the gig as a boat of pleasure'. Another critic regarded the canoe as a 'broad clumsy flat-bottomed funny' and described MacGregor has 'having gradually become a kind of aquatic centaur—his lower part being a boat, and his upper a wandering Englishman'.

During the winter of 1866 John MacGregor pondered over his exploits of the two preceding summers and decided that, all things considered, there were certain limiting factors to canoeing and that the pleasures of a voyage would only be complete if progress was not solely dependent on muscular power, if food could be stored on board and he could sleep afloat. Thereupon he resolved to build a thoroughly good sailing boat—the largest that could be well managed in rough weather by one strong man, a precursor to Francis Chichester's *Gipsy Moth*.

Now it so happened that the Emperor Napoleon III, whose fancy for imitating the English had led him to patronise the introduction into France of English sports, had read of *Rob Roy's* exploits and was anxious to have an exhibition of pleasure boats at the Exposition Universelle of 1867 'to encourage a taste for the exploration of solitary streams and lonely currents among the youth of France'. The boat exhibition was to be followed by a regatta on the Seine. MacGregor was one of the organising committee (which included the Prince of Wales), and decided to sail in a boat of his own to the exhibition with a cargo of Protestant tracts so that at the same time he could organise canoeing events in the regatta, bring the true faith to benighted Roman Catholics and collect material for further lectures and another book, the profits from which should go to the training ship for boys; philanthropic ends would be furthered and another summer boating exhibition justified. The voyage was thus conceived and carried out as a piece of showmanship.

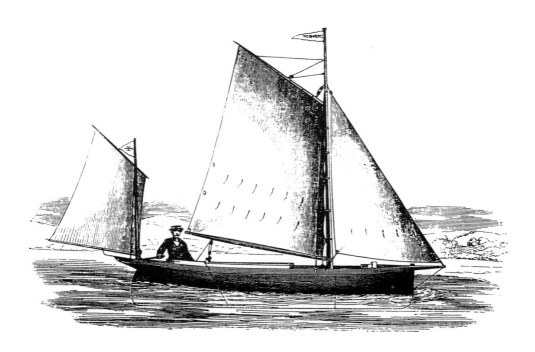

30. The yawl *Rob Roy*. In 1868 MacGregor sailed the yawl from the Thames to Littlehampton via the Wey and Arun Canal recording in his diary that he had had 'adventures in locks'

The yacht was designed by John White of Cowes and built by Forrest of Lime-house, the lifeboat builders. She was 21 feet in length. The first requirement was safety, and this was provided by a seven-foot breadth of beam, a strongly bolted iron Kelson, four watertight compartments and a double skin of Honduras mahogany and yellow pine with canvas in between; an eight-foot dinghy was also carried below deck in the sleeping compartment.

The second need was for comfort, but this was in the Victorian sense of preservation of health, morale and energy; certainly the facilities were cramped; ablutions were carried out by a morning dip or the use of a tin basin. The yawl was fully decked except for an open well, three feet square and deep near the stern, in which there was a seat with a cork cushion and which could be covered with a hatch and rubber tarpaulin in rough weather. In two large leather pockets fixed in the well were the sundries—a long knife, string and cord, an ivory foot ruler and binoculars by Steward in the Strand. On the left of the seat was a door hinged to fall downwards to form a dining table and reveal a cook's dresser holding a flat copper kettle, a copper frying pan and a saucepan, an enamel plate and cutlery; on the right in a similar compartment lay the bread store, tablecloth, butter-keg, biscuit-box, flask of rum, candles, a shiplight and methylated spirits. Inside the cabin beneath the main deck were four boxes labelled 'Dressing', 'Reading and Writing', 'Tools' and 'Eating'. At night, when anchored solely for the purpose, MacGregor slept beneath the main hatch. 'So', wrote the adventurer, 'her internal arrangements for cooking, reading, writing, provisions were quite different from those in any other yacht since they were designed for one-man voyages.'

The *Rob Roy* yawl was launched at Woolwich on 7 June 1867 and a leisurely start made for Paris. From Dover, MacGregor sailed across to Boulogne and then down the French coast to Le Havre. From this port the yawl was towed up river by six different steamers, the last of which was powered by a chain laid along the bottom of the Seine. MacGregor found this part of the voyage very tiring since 'there was no romance in this manner of progress up the river'. Reaching St Cloud on 30 June he prepared the yawl for the French exhibition by painting the inside a Cambridge blue before 'mooring right opposite the sloping sward of the Exhibition'.

Some 30 English and French canoes assembled for the regatta held at the time of the French exhibition. Unfortunately the Emperor, Napoleon III, who 'had given prizes of £1000', did not in the event make an appearance and the Prince of Wales had to remain in London to receive the Sultan of Turkey.

After the regatta, in which MacGregor did not himself participate, was over he set sail downstream but found this difficult work because of the rapid stream, the heavy barge traffic and low height of the Seine bridges which barely allowed the yawl to pass except close to the keystone.

By the time he had reached the junction of the Oise and the Seine he had decided to get a tow down to Le Havre.* Even at Rouen it was difficult to find an anchorage and impossible to get a quiet berth by the quay. Then while being towed beneath the last bridge over the river, the captain, having lowered his funnel, forgot about the yawl and her mast struck the bridge, bent but fortunately did not break. Finally,

---

* P. G. Hamerton later wrote scathingly of Mr MacGregor: 'I need scarcely observe that a house-boat would have been more amusing and incomparably more comfortable' than the yawl which carried so much ballast that it could not be rowed on the Seine (*The Saone A Summer Voyage*, 1887, p. 363).

while anchored overnight by Quilleboeuf she was nearly sunk by being caught between two steamers. After resting a day or so at Le Havre, MacGregor left harbour very early one morning and found himself by chance rather than by intention entering Littlehampton Harbour the following day. He found the *Beach Hotel* very comfortable; the landlady of the good old English type and her son, the waiter, rampant about canoes, and keeping an aviary under the porch and a capital swimming dog in the stable. 'Lie on a sofa in the coffee-room detached, and read *The Times*—go into the drawing room and play piano, or sit under the garden trees and gaze on the fair blue sea, and hope fervently that, with a strong Tory government to protect our institutions, this hotel may be long kept hid from that merciless monster the "Company (Limited)".'

On his arrival at Littlehampton on 24 July* MacGregor had furnished *The Times* with an account of his voyage, so that his craft needed no introduction when he reached Cowes for the Royal Yacht Squadron Regatta. At length the *Rob Roy* returned along the south coast, ventured up the Medway to near Maidstone, ranged several times up and down the Thames before returning to Woolwich on 21 September. For the next six weeks MacGregor worked on *The Voyage Alone in the Yawl Rob Roy* which was published on 14 December. A second edition appeared the following May. Meantime he had lunched at Marlborough House with the Prince of Wales who 'took me into his private rooms and settled letter to the Prince Imperial advising him that he had been made an honorary member of the Royal Canoe Club'.

In June 1868 MacGregor sailed his yawl up the Thames from Erith to enter the Wey Navigation at Weybridge. His diary records: 'June 10th. By Wey River. Adventures in locks', and these doubtless were similar to those that befell Dashwood the previous July (see Chapter VI). No notes were made of his voyage through the Wey & Arun Canal but on the 18th he entered the Arun Navigation and reached Littlehampton the following day.

In July, MacGregor resolved to take his canoe to Egypt and Palestine. On 29 September he paddled his latest *Rob Roy* canoe (the fifth) from Temple Pier to London Bridge where he joined the *Tanjore* bound for Alexandria and Port Said to embark upon what was to be his most celebrated tour. The new 14-foot oak canoe with cedar decking had been built by John Pembury of Mortlake and her top mast had deep blue sails to temper the glare of the sun. MacGregor launched her at the end of October.

The Suez Canal was only partially completed when MacGregor paddled through it from Port Said, probably the first pleasure boat to do so, although steamers, sail launches and Egyptian sailing boats were already using the waterway. Huge dredgers, cranes and elevators plied by steam day and night scooping out sand and mud and piling it on each side in mimic mountains.

At Suez in November 1868 MacGregor met 27-year-old Henry Morton Stanley† of the *New York Herald*, on his way back from Abyssinia, and lent him a copy of *The Voyage Alone*, which so interested Stanley that he told MacGregor he had sat up all night until he had read the book right through. 'He said he would write a regular "stunner" to his paper about canoes and my present voyage, and to give it point would telegraph about my being here to Associated Press, which would be in

---

* A letter dated 25 July [1867] from Littlehampton giving his first account of the crossing from Le Havre was printed as an appendix in the 1954 reprint of *The Voyage Alone*, which contained an introduction by Arthur Ransome.

† *See opp. page.*

five hundred American papers, and put people on tiptoe to hear more! What a sensational set these Yankees are! In return I gave him a short letter of introduction to Dr Livingstone,* and he went off to Aden to meet him and to get first news for America from his own lips—that is to hear if he went round Lake Tanganyika, and so solved the problem of the Nile's source.'

Returning to Port Said, MacGregor took a steamer to Beirut and then went up the Abana and Pharpar rivers. After spending three weeks in Syria, he arrived from Damascus at the source of the Jordan on 6 January. The *Rob Roy* was floated on it for part of its course until rocks forced the canoe to be portaged to tributaries and to Lake Hijaneh, whose edge was bordered by dense papyrus through which MacGregor discovered the Jordan stream flowed.

Lake Hijaneh was covered with reeds 10 feet or more high, 'the largest I obtained was 20 feet, allowing for five feet of immersion . . . These canes were a barrier not easily forced', and had to be steered through by compass.

It was not possible to canoe beyond the Bridge of the Daughters of Jacob since the Jordan's rapid descent to the Sea of Galilee is marked by cataracts and waterfalls. Transporting the canoe over this rough countryside of 'stony hills and dizzy precipices' was hard going. After exploring the lower reaches of the Jordan as far as the ruined bridge of Semakh, a mile-and-a-half distant from the Sea of Galilee, he landed in the Plain of Gennesareth and visited Cana and Nazareth.

31. MacGregor entering the mouth of the river Jordan from Lake Hooleh, 1868

† Stanley had only the previous April achieved his first great scoop by being first with the news of the success of the Napier expedition and the British victory at Magdala. He was in Suez on a routine assignment for the *New York Herald* to check a rumour that Dr Livingstone was about to emerge from Africa at either Suez or Zanzibar following his last expedition which had started early in 1866. In fact it was not until more than five years later that Stanley met Livingstone at Ujiji. MacGregor did not meet Stanley again until 1878, when 'he recognised me as last seeing him at Suez.'

* MacGregor first met David Livingstone the African missionary at his father's house in Dublin in the summer of 1857. MacGregor was much impressed by the heroic pioneer of Christianity and made some sketches for Livingstone's book *Travels and Researches in South Africa*. Later that year he also arranged a reception for him at Cambridge which led to such important ulterior results. Livingstone's last letter to MacGregor was dated 5 February 1858 and explained his plans for opening up the Zambezi to commerce.

Then, as its first explorer, he paddled down the river Kishon, 'a dull river, very hard to get to, over a wide plain of soft sand which was full of crocodiles' to the Mediterranean.

The account of his cruises on the Nile, the Red Sea, the Jordan, the lake of Gennesareth and the water of Damascus was published in November 1869. Before the day of publication 2000 copies of *Rob Roy on the Jordan* were ordered and, within a fortnight, 5000 copies sold. Within 12 months four reprints had been issued and the book continued to be reprinted until 1908.

MacGregor had many hair-breadth escapes in his canoeing expeditions which are vividly detailed in his books. There are pictures of him clenching his teeth and clutching his paddle as the canoe dashes into the rapids of the Reuss, or battling in his frail craft in a fearful storm off Beachy Head or falling overboard in his efforts to save his yawl being smashed by two steamers on the Seine. The most dramatic was when he was sailing along the Jordan pursued by a mob of Hooleh Arabs. After being fired on from the bank, he was taken prisoner by the simple expedient of

32. MacGregor captured by Arabs, 1868

having his canoe and himself lifted bodily out of the water and carried into the presence of the local sheikh. Finding himself a prisoner in danger of his life, he succeeded in escaping with the skilful assistance of Hany, his dragoman, and resumed his cruise.

John MacGregor continued his voyages into the '70s. He spent much of the summer of 1870 with the Canoe Club and canoeing along the south coast from Cowes to Plymouth, Falmouth and the Scilly Isles, observing many German vessels blockaded in port from fear of the French warships in the Channel. The canoe spent that winter in MacGregor's bedroom in the Temple. In August 1871 MacGregor toured the coast and canals of Holland and the Zuyder Zee, made detailed notes but decided his adventures did not warrant a book, although his biographer Edwin Hodder claimed it was one of his most interesting cruises and would have made an exceptionally novel and entertaining book. Certainly, the crowds who turned out to see the canoe expected royalty and at the island of Urk the whole population appeared to be there—hundreds of people wading round and round and standing in thick groups on the piers, the shore and the housetops. Even on this Dutch cruise he had some stirring adventures and on one occasion the *Rob Roy* was nearly sucked into the wake of a large steamer's revolving screw-blades. The following year he was writing in February to the Prince of Wales and the Prince Imperial about the Canoe Club. A cruise to the Crimea was cancelled in favour of one in the Shetland Islands.

In 1873 he planned a trip to the Azores but at the last moment changed his mind about taking his canoe and while at Terceira decided on 25 August to marry Annie Caffin whom he had 'loved eight years in silence'. On 4 December he was married at Blackheath. His canoe exploits were over. Instead he began and carried out a series of extremely successful lecture tours to raise money for boys' charities. During 1870 he gave 56 'Rob Roy' lectures earning £4,160 and by 1878 he had succeeded in reaching his target of £10,000 free of expenses, a sum which he donated to the various missions and societies with which he was involved (e.g., the Shoeblacks, Shipwrecked Mariners, and National Lifeboat Institution, etc.). He died in July 1892 aged 67 after a long and debilitating illness.

Although best known for his canoeing exploits, MacGregor's greatest achievements arose from the help he gave to the waifs and strays of London. His influence with young men of all classes was remarkable. His ready sympathy with their difficulties coupled with his own manly character and pursuits won their admiration. His canoe exploits were the outcome of a strong and aspiring nature rather than a restless disposition and gave him the opportunity to spread his missionary faith to a widespread audience, even to the extent that he carried tracts written in French and German in his canoe to pass to those he met. Certainly MacGregor was a remarkable man who lived a life of patient well-doing.

Chapter V

P. G. HAMERTON AND THE UNKNOWN RIVER (1866)

Philip Hamerton—early life—marriage—moves to France—his voyage on the Arroux in a paper canoe—publication of The Unknown River *in the* Fortnightly Review *(1867)—portfolio of etchings sold by Colnaghi—reprinted in* The Portfolio *(1869)—revised edition in book form (1871)—American edition (1872).*

MOST MEMBERS made rather less publicised voyages than did the Captain of the Canoe Club. One of the least heralded was made in France in a paper canoe. It so happened that amongst those who joined the club in 1866 was Philip Hamerton, then aged 32, who was to become from 1869 until his death in 1894 the editor of *The Portfolio*, a distinguished art periodical.

Hamerton was born in Lancashire. His mother died before he was 12 months old and his father, who was an alcoholic and treated his son pretty badly, died seven years later. The young orphan was brought up by an aunt and educated at Burnley; later he studied painting under J. Pettie and sought advice from John Ruskin.

Hamerton was an eccentric character. In 1857 he rented a farmhouse on the solitary 30-acre islet of Innistrynich on Loch Awe. Here he delighted in the rugged scenery with its lakes, mountains and wild moorland, especially 'the dark waters of Loch Awe when they dashed in spray on the rocks of some lovely islet and his boat flew past in the grey and dreary gloaming'.[20] In particular he loved camping, boating and sketching.

In May 1858 he married a young French girl, Eugenie Gindriez, whom he·had first met two years before at her father's house in Paris. Returning from Paris after the wedding they went straight from London to Glasgow and thence to Loch Awe 'which happened at that time to be enveloped in a dense fog that lasted two days'. To the dismay of his young wife nothing was visible but a still grey shoreless sea. His 18-year-old bride, with only a smattering of English, was not a little daunted at the primitiveness and isolation of her husband's home, which she described as 'rich in surprises to my foreign notions'. Nevertheless, they had two servants and it was not long before a third and a fourth was hired. The purchase of two cows, a small flock of sheep, poultry and the cultivation of a vegetable plot soon followed.

Such nuptial bliss was soon threatened, however, by the financial burdens of living in so isolated a manner, and Hamerton was persuaded to move to France and finally found in 1862 a charming property near Autun in Burgundy. In the same year Hamerton's first book, *A Painter's Camp in the Highlands*, was published and achieved an immediate success in both England and America. He started contributing to the 'Fortnightly' and other reviews, wrote two novels and in 1869 founded *The Portfolio*.

33. Philip Hamerton (1834–94)

Hamerton's house at Pré-Charmoi was bordered by the shallow winding Ternin stream, on which he experimented with the canoes he built. Through Autun, however, flowed the Arroux, a tributary of the Loire, which he wished to explore and which 'united all the charms of lovely scenery, picturesque architecture and adventure, and perfect novelty for no human being had ever attempted the descent of it in a boat'. He had a joiner knock up a skeleton canoe frame which he covered with several thicknesses of stout waterproof paper stuck together with a kind of mastic,

known as the 'enduit Ruolz' after its inventor, the celebrated chemist.* The canoe
had a paper deck, and in spite of its flimsiness, proved a serviceable craft, although
she drew rather too much water and turned rather too easily.

One purpose of the voyage was to provide etchings of the scenery; consequently
progress was exceedingly slow and would have wearied any companions other than
Tom, his large dog, 'who swam nearly the whole distance behind the boat, down the
rapids and everywhere'. However, Hamerton explained his enjoyment of venturing
on an unknown European river as being the assurance of 'finding much that is worth
finding, and of enjoying many of the sensations which give interest to more famous
explorations'; and he added, 'it is necessary to the complete enjoyment of an excursion of discovery that the region to be explored, whether mountain or river,
should not have been already explored by others, or at any rate not with the same
objects and intentions'.[21]

The expedition began on a fine autumn afternoon in 1866 with the *Jenny* being
carted to the banks of the river at Voudenay le Chateau, where he spent the night
at the village inn. Hamerton paddled off smoothly enough next morning since the
stream, though narrow, was unencumbered by trees; soon, however, it became lined
with thick willows and the passage had to be made through a sylvan tunnel three or
four feet wide. A fallen tree trunk, tangled vegetation and some very sharp corners

34. Hamerton in his paper canoe, 1866

caused delays, the sinking of the canoe and eventually a portage over a field. By the
end of the first day one mile had been covered and the night was spent at the inn at
Voudenay l'Eglise where he shared a bedroom with the innkeeper and his apprentice.
Because the stream was impassable the canoe had to be carted the next morning two
or three miles before being relaunched. From this point an hour's travel down the
narrow and tortuous river brought Hamerton to the round and square towers of the

* To his American readers Hamerton confessed (1872) that the 'enduit Ruolz' took about 12 months to harden
and so, lacking that amount of time, the paper did not really adhere and the water oozed in after a while.

35. Portaging across the fields

castle of Igornay, which he spent five hours sketching. Then the canoe had to be portaged over the mill-weir and dragged over the shallows, but the swift current soon carried him down to the rapids at the foot of a steeply-wooded hill.* No sooner was the white water successfully overcome than Hamerton was knocked into the river as the boat passed under a fallen tree. His box of etching plates remained

36. The castle of Igornay on the river Arroux

*The author retraced Hamerton's route on foot and by boat and found it little altered except that in August 1977 the swift current beyond Igornay was not so noticeable. In 1977 this part of the river was then so overgrown that it took 6 hours to cover 2 miles.

afloat so that, by the time he had baled out, refloated his canoe and recaptured his possessions, the total loss amounted to a pair of shoes, a hat, a sponge and a pair of socks.

A mile further on Hamerton was able to change his clothes at the next mill, where his experiences had all the makings of a French nouvelle, but which are related without innuendo. Apparently the house had only one room with four beds and a little table in the middle; the floor was of clay and rather dirty, but in spite of this he begged a night's lodging which the miller's wife granted cheerfully enough; 'the good woman took clean coarse canvas sheets out of her cupboard, and put them on her best bed. There was only one bedroom, it is true, for all of us, male and female, but at least I had a whole bed to myself'. In the middle of the night Hamerton awoke and saw 'by the dim light of a lamp a sour-visaged man with a great scimitar-like knife in his hand. He was drunk and alternating between fits of sullen silence and loud fury'. This turned out to be the master of the house just returned from market, whose Morvandean patois was unintelligible to Hamerton. Nevertheless, surmising that he was the cause of all the trouble, he bravely confronted the husband who concluded the scene by vilifying his wife and deciding to spend the night in an outhouse. Hamerton calmly went back to sleep on his own bed, but rose early the next morning, and finding that he was only seven miles from home, borrowed a horse and cart and returned thither to repair his previous day's losses.*

On resuming the paddle in the brilliant light of a new a cloudless day, Hamerton found the narrowness of the stream continued to present problems and it was not long before he was clinging to the branch of a tree while the canoe filled rapidly. One factor which annoyed him was the groups of people who stood on the river's bank and stared at his tiny craft and greeted him with roars of laughter. However, he wisely commented that 'these are to be endured philosophically as every landscape painter knows'. After rushing through many more narrow passages between thick growths of willow, the confluence of the Arroux and Drée was reached. 'The river was now a constant succession of beautiful broad pools linked together by rapid babbling shallows, over which the canoe darted gaily and swiftly without grounding.'

At length a winding of the beautiful river disclosed Autun 'on the slope of a lofty hill blue in the haze of the bright afternoon, with massive walls and many towers', old Augustodunum, whose Roman fortifications now enclosed the vegetables of market gardeners. As the canoe glided under the bridge, Hamerton noticed on the right that two of the four walls of the tower known as the Temple of Janus, though pierced with jagged openings, still stood. Two tributaries [a stream from the Bois de Montepauvoise and the Ternin] joined the Arroux under the city walls, but further on a suspension bridge had been carried away by a recent flood which made the stream impassable and necessitated a portage. This delay, increased by a voluntary stoppage of four hours while Hamerton etched 'a very tempting subject', caused him to be still afloat in the dark on a rapid broad and stony stream six miles from the nearest village. So this night was spent on the river bank inside his narrow canoe into which he had strewn rushes and placed a woollen sack.

On the following morning Hamerton etched the castle of Chaseux, a picturesque ruin by the river, whose towers he considered were remarkably tiny for a feudal work.

* In later versions this incident was glossed over, and in *The Unknown River* he merely stated: 'After a night's rest in a poor cottage, the voyage was resumed in the brilliant light of a new and cloudless day'.

At the little village of Étang, which had two fine bridges and a railway station just built, he found the old houses near the river a good subject for etching. A day was also spent exploring the Beuvray and the hill of Uchon which not only carried on its rocky height a tall fragment of a medieval castle, but a rocking stone—La Pierre qui Croule—which had resisted all efforts by the local peasants to be moved from its pivot.

Reaching Laisy next day Hamerton shared a bedroom with a young farmer at the inn, and spent much time sketching; he also found himself dancing with the bride at a village wedding 'whirling about on a rough stone floor in thick boots to the sound of a villainous hurdy-gurdy'.

Resuming his voyage, he passed through beautiful scenery and arrived that evening at St Nizier, a very quaint little village with a tiny disused Romanesque church which was filled with straw. He slept in the public room of the inn which had been under water in the flood and very damp. However, the fare was simple but sufficient, the bed good and clean and he 'found one or two amusing books, especially Edouard Charton's *History of France*'.

Many noble trees stood around St Nizier, including an oak whose girth was 50 feet. There were fine rocky foregrounds, too, and plenty of gorse which delayed

37. The oak tree at St Nizier

Hamerton's departure for Blot—a hamlet built on a rocky promontory where he also stopped to etch. At Laboulaye he hid the boat and walked on to Toulon-sur-Arroux, a picturesque little town whose *maire* was the principal innkeeper, 'a man of great reputation as a cook and maker of pastry, and the most irascible little gentleman in the world'. The river from Laboulaye to Toulon was so delightful that Hamerton, while staying in Toulon, paddled only a mile or so a day 'through beautiful woods and rocky passes', and then returned to the village each day to continue his drawing. At one point the Arroux expanded into a long narrow lake with an islet in the middle with shores of rock and fern. A mill stood at one end whose weir Hamerton discended safely, and then at Toulon he tried the more difficult leap of a cascade. 'The boat was tossed like a feather on the curling crests of the permanent waves and shot down the rapid like a sleigh going down a hill of ice.' Plenty of water came over the deck but only his arms got wet.

A day or two later an untoward accident caused him to break a paddle and he had to row the eight miles to Gueugnon using only half. Stones in the river bed had caused a leak and this was repaired by a 'clever' joiner who also made him two paddles. At Gueugnon a young man showed him his pleasure boat—a narrow, flat-bottomed iron structure, very easily upset and not in some respects ill-adapted for river work. On leaving the town he lost his dog which had returned to the inn where he had been staying, and after spending a disconsolate day, had found his way home more than thirty miles away where he had arrived exhausted. It was a severe run, for no doubt he had made the distance double by following the river and 'often I daresay swimming against the stream. I never knew such a persistent swimmer. He never had the sense to follow the canoe on the bank but would always swim behind it, however cold the water or long the distance. It was this which had separated him from me. Being in a hurry I had pushed on too fast.'

Finally, after a long paddle in clear magnificent moonlight 'which gave an indescribable poetry and enchantment to every turn of the river', Hamerton's paper canoe floated triumphantly on to the broad waters of the Loire at Digoin.

It was the *Fortnightly Review* which in February 1867 printed Hamerton's account of his 'Canoe Voyage' on the Arroux, but he revised the text and republished it in serial form with etchings printed on India paper and mounted on the text in the first volume of *The Portfolio* in 1869.

A critic in the *Athenaeum* accused the author of 'intense egotism' and another complained that he 'talked too much about his dog'. To these criticisms Hamerton replied that if the story of the voyage is to be faithfully narrated, how was he to tell the tale and that if you listened to critics you would never publish anything. He may well, however, have listened to his wife when the book came to be published for he omits the details of the incident when he spent the night in the cottage near Autun in the same room as the miller's wife.

Thirty-six etchings, contained in a portfolio designed by John Leighton, were also published in six monthly parts by Colnaghi in 1867. Hamerton dedicated these etchings to 'the Captain and Members of the Canoe Club'. Each number cost half a guinea and the complete portfolio three guineas.

It had been Hamerton's intention to publish his account in book form with additional illustrations and in July 1870 he began making larger plates intending to revisit the scenery of the whole river, but with the French defeated at Sedan and the Emperor Napoleon III deposed on 4 September, spy fever seized France. Hamerton had to give up the idea 'for it is not safe in this month of September 1870 to draw so much as a wicket-gate of a cottage garden anywhere in France'.[22]

A CANOE

VOYAGE

ETCHINGS

BY

PHILIP GILBERT HAMERTON

DEDICATED TO HIS BRETHREN OF THE CANOE CLUB

IN SIX MONTHLY PARTS

EACH PART CONTAINING SIX ETCHINGS

PART 1

NOTE. — The price of each number is half a guinea.
The numbers are sold separately.   Subscribers to the whole work receive the earliest impressions and a portfolio by LEIGHTON.
The etchings are printed by AUGUSTE DELATRE, 303, rue Saint-Jacques, Paris.

LONDON

PAUL & DOMINIC COLNAGHI & Cᵒ

14 — PALL MALL EAST — 14

1867

38. Cover design for Hamerton's etchings of *A Canoe Voyage*, 1867

THE

UNKNOWN

R·I·V·E·R

BY

PHILIP GILBERT HAMERTON.

Illustrated by the Author.

39. Title page for the first edition of *The Unknown River*, 1871, depicting the gate-tower at Chaseux on the river Arroux

The Unknown River, an Etcher's Voyage of Discovery appeared in 1871, elegantly bound in gilt-decorated blue cloth with all edges gilt and 37 etchings at a price of 15 shillings. The reviews were mixed. *The Times* critic magnanimously wrote 'The book has pleased us and we are sure it will please our readers'. The *Pall Mall Gazette* thought the letter press should allure many readers while the *Guardian* rather whimsically wrote 'We take up this highly attractive volume with a smile and cannot lay it down without a sigh. *The Unknown River* is a share in the misfortuntes of France'.

The book was also published by Robert Brothers of Boston in 1872 who reported that it had proved a success and had been generally admired. 'It is a charming book and we should like to bring out a popular edition.' Seeley's published an octavo edition in 1874 with only eight illustrations. The first edition was advertised at the back as still being available so the numbers sold were probably relatively few. Nevertheless, the story of this canoe voyage appeared no less than five times in print.

Chapter VI

MR AND MRS DASHWOOD'S TRIP FROM THE THAMES
TO THE SOLENT (1867)

A family holiday—purpose of voyage—fitting out—the Wey Navigation—Guildford—shallows at Shalford—charged by oxen—the Wey & Arun Junction Canal—bad news at Bramley— return to Guildford—voyage continued—picnic lunch at Loxwood—comfortable night at Billingshurst—Pallingham Lock—Mrs Dashwood in danger at Hardham—the canal tunnel— against the tide to Arundel—Littlehampton—sea voyage to Lymington.

THE PUBLICATION in 1868 of *The Thames to the Solent by Canal and Sea or the Log of the Una Boat 'Caprice'* heralded a new dimension to pleasure boat literature. It is, indeed, the first account of a family outing and it was written by J. B. Dashwood with the intention of making known a novel way of spending a holiday afloat.

Dashwood's plan was to voyage up the Wey Navigation to Shalford, proceed through the Wey & Arun Junction Canal and the Arun Navigation and join the river Arun at Coldwaltham. At Ford they hoped to enter the Portsmouth & Arundel Canal which would allow them to reach Lymington with only a short sea voyage from Portsmouth. That this route could not be accomplished in its entirety was not discovered until they had nearly crossed into Sussex. There were other frustrations, too, in the shape of numerous gates across the towpath, and locks whose opening was a most laborious process. There were also occasions for alarm when the *Caprice* was threatened by a herd of charging oxen outside Guildford, nearly sunk in Hardham Lock and almost swamped in the Solent.

No pre-arranged plans were made for accommodation, nor did they plan to camp out. In this respect they were generally very fortunate in finding hotels and inns which provided excellent board and lodging. The story of their adventure can be summarily recounted as follows.

On 8 July 1867 Dashwood set off from Weybridge in sunny weather, accompanied by his wife and dog, to watch the naval review being held at Spithead in honour of the Sultan of Turkey's state visit. An odd assortment of stores had been loaded on board, which included rugs, umbrellas, cooking apparatus, a large hamper, a ship's compass, a keg of beer, and an india-rubber bath. The low clearance of many of the bridges had necessitated the substitution of a 7-foot towing mast for the 20-foot mast (which was lashed to the boom), while a pony and groom had been hired to tow the boat.

At Thames lock the toll of 5s. was paid to Guildford, and a 'most civil and obliging' lock-keeper provided them with a 3-foot-long crowbar for opening the locks. On the Wey the lock paddles were placed in the centre of the gates so that it was necessary to insert the point of the crowbar in the teeth of the paddle-bar while sitting astride the gates and, by a series of violent jerks, raise it inch by inch. Most of the hatches were very stiff and difficult to raise or lower, and since success

40. Dashwood working a lock on the Wey Navigation, 1867

depended on good leverage, the crowbar had to be worked from the extreme end of the handle so that if the point slipped out of the niche while the wrench was being made, away went the user headlong into the water. No mishaps occurred on this voyage, but the fruits of Dashwood's labours were a not inconsiderable number of cuts and bruises.

Leaving Weybridge, the party traversed a long avenue lined with tall alders and spanned by rustic bridges. 'The day was hot and the cool shade most refreshing; the banks were covered with luxuriant ferns and wild flowers, and the white and yellow waterlilies, floating on the smooth surface of the water, lent enchantment to the view.' Emerging upon Newhaw lock, they came up with a barge, whose crew offered them their services, which they readily accepted, and so ascended together into a more open country of meadowland and cornfields (one of the few references to barges during the voyage). Admiring the woodlands of St George's Hill, they soon sighted West Hall Lodge, where an enthralling game of croquet was in progress. Passing Wisley Common and the ruins of Newark Priory, they procured bread and cheese and drank beer with the weary haymakers at the little inn by Pyrford lock. Proceeding through Walsam and Peppercourt locks, they lunched by the water's edge at Send before reaching Triggs lock and the grounds of Sutton Place, the former home of Sir Richard Weston (also more recently of the Duke of Sutherland and the late Mr Paul Getty). By now the day was far advanced and the great heat had given place to a calm and lovely evening. 'We glided along the banks gay with water-iris, both yellow and blue, the pretty little forget-me-nots in quantities, the large yellow ranunculus, with no end of other pretty wild flowers, the air fragrant with the scent of new mown hay and the delicious smelling meadow-sweet.'

Beyond Bowers lock the voyagers entered Stoke Park and at the flour mill showed their way-bill to the toll-keeper. Then, as night was falling, Guildford was reached. The town was alive with excitement as the Foresters' Fête was in progress with the bands of Volunteers parading the streets in every direction. Mooring *Caprice* under the bridge, they left her in charge of the boatman on the quay and spent the night at the *White Lion*.

Leaving the town early next morning their enthusiasm was dampened at the sight of a small screw steamer just arrived from Brighton, lying thoroughly disabled. It appeared that the weeds on the lower part of the canal had been so thick that they had completely fouled her screw and, to make matters worse, she had burst her boilers. However, Dashwood consoled himself with the thought that he could penetrate where the steamer had cleared a passage and was relieved to find that the new series of locks could be operated with a windlass from 'terra firma', although the hatches remained terribly stiff.

The first serious check to their journey occurred at St Catherine's lock. Some hundred yards after passing through the upper gates *Caprice* stuck fast in the mud in less than a foot of water. Unable to move or to land, the party were espied in their dilemma by an old lady, who informed them that they had no business to be there as the water had been let off for nine days to effect mill repairs. Dashwood pleaded their plight and she, becoming more amiable, told them where they might find the lock-keeper who alone could help. Sitting under umbrellas in the broiling sun while their groom went off to find him, some alarm was occasioned by a large herd of 'formidable-looking oxen' in the adjoining meadow who, drawing themselves up in line, 'charged down upon us with lowered heads and tails erect, threatening us

41. The Dashwoods in an alarming position near St Catherine's lock, Guildford, Surrey

with instant annihilation'. But, as Dashwood says, the animals, on reaching the bank, were almost as astonished as they were to find the river empty and, after much snorting, turned away.

Eventually, the couple were released from their predicament (half-a-crown did the trick), but already it was too late for them to reach Loxwood that night. At Shalford a toll of 1s. was paid to the Godalming Navigation and at Stonebridge they entered the Wey & Arun, where the water was again very shallow. However, they had just sufficient draught to enter the first lock and, passing the large tanyard at Gosden and two more locks, they reached Bramley wharf, where they met William Stanton, the 'good-natured superintendent of the canal at the Guildford end, and a coal-merchant whose barges travelled regularly between London, Bramley and Little-hampton'. Stanton told Dashwood all about the Wey & Arun and offered the party 'the run of his kitchen garden, rich in gooseberries and currants'.

However, they also learnt to their dismay that the Ford section of the Portsmouth & Arundel Canal no longer existed (the last boat had passed through at least ten years before). In consequence of this discovery and in view of the hazards of taking such a frail craft into the open sea (the bulwarks rose only 6 ins. above water), they decided, after much deliberation, to return to Guildford, only to run aground again in the shallows at Shalford. While waiting for more water to be released, a passing bargee's encouragement and the toss of a coin caused them to change their minds and return to Bramley, where they planned to spend the night. 'In process of time we got to Bramley once more, much to the surprise of Mr Stanton and the natives. It was too late to proceed further so we deposited our goods in safe keeping in Mr Stanton's stores and set out in search of dinner and a lodging for the night.' However, fresh difficulties beset them, for no suitable accommodation was to be found and they had to take the train to Guildford. The *Grantley Arms* at Wonersh clearly displeased them, for it was referred to as a 'pokey little inn', while the *White Hart* was described as 'the best hotel in Guildford, where we regaled ourselves with a capital dinner and were thankful that we were not in the *Grantley Arms*'.

The fourth chapter described their third day's trip from Bramley to Newbridge. In consequence of the shortage of water in the canal and the Company's new rule regarding pleasure craft, they had to take with them George Cox, a 19-year-old bargee, who worked for Stanton. The toll to Newbridge was 5s. and there was in addition the pilot's fee of 10s. to be paid. The weather continued fine, and the scenery beyond Bramley and through Lord Grantley's property, where the canal wound its way under the shade of woods reaching down to the water's edge, was greatly praised. Many of the bridges had a bare 7 feet headroom and the small iron drawbridge at Whipley Manor had to be opened. However, their pace was quickened by the forethought of young Cox, who ran ahead, in spite of the heat of a broiling sun, to prepare the locks. Only the double swing gates hampered their progress; as they were impossible to ride through, the groom had to dismount at almost every field to free the tow-rope. After passing heather-covered common and water-meadows, the party entered the summit cutting, which was dug through great oak plantations and spanned by a series of low stone bridges. On reaching Sidney Wood, they wended their way 'through a most refreshing and picturesque country of a

42. Low bridges on the Wey & Arun Junction Canal which linked the Thames to
the English Channel. It was closed in 1871

broken and undulating character, densely clothed with a forest of oak trees, opening
out and giving peeps into deep hollows verdant with luxuriant ferns and purple
heather. Here and there were breaks in the woodland, and the small round hills, rich
in pasturage, appeared—the ancient folds of the Weald. We now commenced to make
our descent towards the sea, and lock after lock followed each other in rapid succession.' At half past one they reached Loxwood and noted the 'neat clean little inn
[The *Onslow Arms*] close by the canalside'. However, the decision to take lunch
'al fresco' in the shade of a big oak (eating meat pies of doubtful content bought
at Guildford), gave Dashwood the opportunity of observing an unusual way of
catching fish. 'Whilst I was quietly enjoying my pipe after lunch, my curiosity was
raised by seeing a man amusing himself throwing a large stone into the canal attached
to a long line, which he hauled in and flung back over and over again. On approaching him, I soon discovered his little dodge, for I beheld a number of small branches
floating about in all directions, to which fine-gut lines and hooks were attached,
wherewith to ensnare the wily fish, somewhat on the principle of the trimmer.
These boughs he got to land by means of his stone, which he flung over them,
drawing them slowly ashore. I did not see him catch anything, although I watched
him for some time; but he assured me he had been very successful by this plan, and
had at times secured pike and other fish of a large size.'

Pressing forward to Newbridge, the countryside was felt to be 'decidedly ugly,
with flat water-meadows on either side', an opinion that could hardly be substantiated by its present-day appearance. The canal was exceedingly weedy as they neared
Rowner lock, and it was necessary to stand forward to clear the bows. Cox, who had
been of the greatest assistance, disembarked at the lock and went off back to Bramley.

Newbridge was reached at half past five, where they anchored and set off on foot to Billingshurst, 1½ miles away, to spend the night at the *King's Arms*. Its hospitality appeared to leave nothing to be desired. Dashwood was full of praise for this neat, clean inn where 'everything was fresh and good of its kind; eggs, butter, bread, fruit, cream, all excellent; and our mutton-chops done to a turn, with excellent beer and very fair sherry'.

Next morning Dashwood was awake at half past four and roused the house in order to make an early start, for the first ripples of the ebb tide would be felt at Coldwaltham lock by noon. 'After a bit the little inn was in a hustle—hot and cold water for shaving, and baths, to any amount, and boots polished like mirrors.' A capital breakfast, followed by a brisk walk to Newbridge, and they were off again by seven. The fine weather continued. At Orfold lock no mention was made of the aqueduct, but the lock-keeper's wife and her two pretty daughters were observed making butter. The *Oarsman's Guide* stated that slight refreshment might be obtained here, 'scanty accommodation also, but to a very limited extent'.[23] Indeed, as the lockhouse had only two tiny bedrooms in which a family of four or more was housed, the traveller would have been lucky to have obtained a chair in the parlour.

Dashwood now found the flat meadows and the scenery more to his liking, although substantially the same as that described as 'decidedly ugly'. The early morning sunshine, the meadows dotted with cattle, the larks in full song, and the canal banks clothed with flowers of every hue and colour accounted perhaps for the difference in outlook. At length the 'great Pallingham lock' was reached, the largest he ever saw—'about 40 feet long and 30 feet deep and wide enough for two good sized barges to lie alongside each other'. Inaccurate, of course, but Dashwood was no judge of distance and, as he had had to fill the basin single-handed, the exaggeration was perhaps understandable. A shilling toll was paid at the lock house—referred to as the receiving-house of the Arun Canal Company, which they learnt was still paying its way in spite of the railway, and formerly produced a very comfortable dividend. Into the Arun proper, and after a couple of miles Stopham bridge was passed. To avoid the detour around Pulborough, they took the short cut to Coldwaltham. However, at Hardham lock the boat nearly sank with Mrs Dashwood on board, when it became wedged under the iron footbridge as the lock was being filled. 'The groom's timely warning saved the day.' Dashwood punted *Caprice* through Hardham tunnel by pushing the boat-hook against the roof. 'In the middle it became quite dark, and we could only just guide ourselves by means of the bright outlet at the end. The roof was covered with stalactites, and in places the water fell upon us from crevices above in heavy drops, so that we had to try to steer clear of them where we heard their splashes on the water below.' After passing through this subterranean passage in about 10 minutes, they had to wait for their groom who, having had to lead the pony over the top as there was no towpath through the tunnel, had mistaken his way. However, by half past twelve they had come upon the last lock at Coldwaltham, where they found the tide had begun to ebb.

Thereafter, great difficulty was experienced in persuading their pony to pass several obnoxious swing gates, three-barred and weighted, and the delay meant that it was nearly 2 o'clock before they reached Amberley; but even so, they made

43. Obnoxious gates along the tow-path of the Arun Navigation

a brief halt to visit the castle. The towing-path ceased at Houghton and, while the groom and pony went on to Arundel by road, they were forced to row the remaining eight miles to the town, partly against the tide. 'The tide was running strong when we passed under the old bridge at Amberley, eating our luncheon as we drifted on. We went by Bury Hill, at a great pace, and soon came to the overhanging wooded cliffs of Arundel Park. The river is here strikingly pretty, and we met a great number of pleasure boats rowing and fishing . . . We soon left the shelter of the woods, the river winding out into the plain, with high mudbanks on each side of us, covered with extensive beds of tall growing sedges. The tide soon began to work up the centre of the river, and we had to hug the banks to try and cheat it. It was now becoming hard work.'

A mile from Arundel they met some barges coming up with the tide and were rejoined by their groom—'we flung him a towing-rope and made him pull us up to the bridge'. Then, after several unsuccessful attempts against the force of the tide, *Caprice* was hauled under Arundel bridge by means of a boat-hook and tied up at the quay.

The last stage of their journey to the sea now commenced, with the pony towing them towards Littlehampton. 'The appearance of the river now showed us that we were evidently approaching the sea. Its great width, the shipping in the distance, and the number of small craft of every description dotted about—some busy fishing and some anchored, some under sail—presented a very animated appearance.'

Cautioned against the chains of the floating bridge, they reached Littlehampton at about half past eight and spent the night at a small riverside inn. 'Our trip by canal', wrote Dashwood, 'had been quite charming but rather hard work.' The total sailing time taken to cover the 62 miles from Weybridge to Littlehampton during the four days was about 28–30 hours, in the course of which they passed through 43 locks and were charged 22s. in tolls and pilots' fees.

Dashwood interviewed a prospective skipper to pilot the boat through the Channel and the Solent. 'He appeared somewhat unsteady on his pins, hummed and hawed a great deal and said he did not much like the job, that he had been out all day fishing off Selsea Bill, that there had been a nasty bumpy sea which would be almost too much for our boat and that he could not think of undertaking the "voyage" with a lady aboard.' However, the skipper changed his mind the next morning and, with a steady breeze, *Caprice* made eight knots towards Portsmouth.

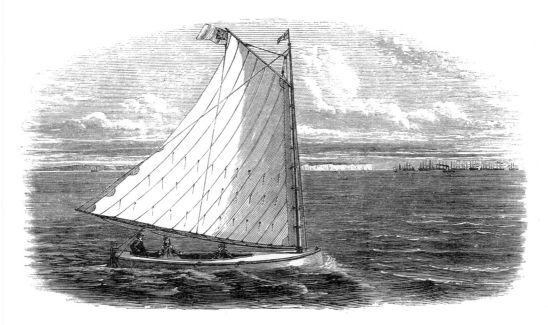

44. The Una boat *Caprice*

The sixth chapter described their hazardous journey by sea to the Solent and the imposing sight of the Fleet off Spithead, while the last was devoted to describing the capabilities and rigging of una boats.

In conclusion, Dashwood thanked his readers for their perseverance in perusing his 'little tale' and hoped that it might encourage those who possessed a small sailing-boat to spend a holiday in this way without much expenditure of either time or money. But in the same year as Dashwood's book was published the Act of abandonment was passed and, within four years of his voyage, the Wey & Arun Junction Canal was closed.

Details of the life and profession of J. Bacon Dashwood are sketchy. His home was at Christchurch, but as his work 'called him to spend his existence within daily reach of London', he also lived on the banks of the Thames. Yachting was his hobby. He owned a fore-and-aft boat for bad weather and a una boat for fine weather sailing. He also enjoyed fishing for mackerel and whiting off Hengistbury Head.

Besides the account of his voyage to the Solent he also produced *The Scholar's Assistant and Standard Table Book*, published by Dashwood Bros. and Charles H. Law of London in 1856. This sixpenny, 47-page booklet contained arithmetical tables, measurements, conversions, foreign currencies and useful information, like the dates of the kings and queens of England.

Those interested in the history of the lost waterway between London and the English Channel are indeed grateful that Dashwood had his log published. Little would he have dreamt that more than a century later it would be reprinted by Shepperton Swan for a wider readership.

Chapter VII

A VOYAGE BY CANOE AND SKIFF FROM MANCHESTER TO LONDON (1868)

Object of voyage—details of stores carried—dress of crew—Bridgewater Canal basin—the Mersey—Ellesmere Canal—help from bargees—the Perry and the Severn—toll charges on the Stroudwater and Thames & Severn Canals—the Upper Thames—arrival at Cannon Street Railway Bridge.

THERE WAS NOTHING particularly heroic or exciting about journeying by canal in the 19th century. In most cases enjoyment was marred by the need to pass innumerable locks and to avoid obstructing commercial traffic, which even in England was quite considerable on most waterways until the 1860s and on many till the end of the century. It was also a fact that many canals could offer little of scenic interest compared with rivers and that tolls for pleasure craft were pretty stiff. These are the main reasons why so little was written in way of personal reminiscences about canal trips. This chapter exemplifies the problems.

The fervour enjoined by the reading of MacGregor's exploits prompted many young men to plan and undertake adventurous voyages overseas. For many, however, the cost was prohibitive and so in the summer of 1868 three individuals decided to venture upon their native waterways and record their experiences 'to inspire those who can't reach the Red Sea, Nile or Jordan, or even the Danube, Rhine and Seine'. Their rather uneventful but pleasantly illustrated account, entitled *The Waterway to London as Explored in the Wanderer and Ranger with Sail, Paddle, and Oar, in a Voyage on the Mersey, Perry, Severn and Thames, and Several Canals*, was published anonymously by Simpkin, Marshall & Co. of Manchester the following year.

The charm of the voyage for the participants was that they could explore at their leisure those hidden beauties visible only from the water which 'must have existed year after year without having gladdened a single heart', but for the reader the narrative is of little interest. It does, however, draw attention to the 'indifference or unhelpful attitude of some canal companies and the Thames Conservancy towards users of pleasure boats and the heavy tolls charged'.

The 500-mile voyage began at the Bridgewater Canal basin in Manchester on a fine Monday morning in August. Loaded on board the 24-foot-long skiff, *Wanderer*, was a cooking lamp, butter keg (four inches square), one enamelled iron cup and three plates and basins, one milk jug, one Etna, one bottle of sauce, medicine chest and sailmaker's and tailor's stores consisting of two needles, six pins, two buttons and some thread on a cork. The 16-foot pine canoe, the *Ranger*, carried waterproof bags containing the stores including a 'formidable piece of bacon'. The three men,

Harry, Will and the author, all wore grey flannel peajackets, white jerseys and knickerbockers, together with white straw hats with blue ribbon. There was also Charlie, a rough-haired yellow terrier.

For the first half hour of their journey they met an endless succession of canal boats 'some with one horse, some with two and others with a trio of donkeys'. At the famous Barton aqueduct they lifted their boats out of the canal, put them into the Mersey and soon were pushing the *Wanderer* over some shallows. 'An hour or two of doubling and twisting in a most bewildering manner between high banks crowned with never-ending orchards soon gave us (in spite of sundry apples and pears) an unmistakable appetite'; so, having sought a farmhouse for bread and water, but finding only water 'we fortunately had some cake on board, and with the aid of our boil-a-quart-of-water-in-three-minutes-lamp, commenced breakfast at 11.30, reclining at an angle of forty five degrees on a steep bank, a rug for the table-cloth, and each with a large pocket-knife, and a still larger appetitie. The rich diet of cold boiled bacon and cake and a cup or two of chocolate soon satisfied our cravings.'[24]

By 4 p.m. they had reached the junction with the Irwell and found the water of the Mersey as black as ink with a high mudbank shutting out the view. Two miles below the weir at Partington, they dined on beef, bacon and 'some excellent claret'. The river now became more attractive. 'A richly wooded bank with fine elms forms an admirable back-ground to the light pine canoe, with its pretty blue flag, gliding along, paddled by the steward, who, with sinewy arms and untiring energy, gave stroke after stroke with the regularity of a steam engine.' A little above Warrington they turned up the canal to Runcorn and, as both night and rain were falling, they stopped at the first bridge and walked a mile or so to a small village where they had to sleep three in a bed. 'We were not long, but before undressing it was a pleasure, after the day of hard toil, to sit down and quietly read a few words from "the Book". And I can say from experience, that a sure way of increasing the pleasure of any excursion my readers may undertake is to get into the habit, before going to bed at night, and before starting in the morning, of reading a few words of the Bible together, and thanking God for all His Goodness, and praying for a continuance of His protecting care.'[25]

By six the next morning they were well along the canal, and by 8.30 were some miles above the town of Runcorn where they rejoined the Mersey. Runcorn they thought a peculiarly dirty and dingy looking town. 'The air was heavy with the smoke of a thousand busy factories.' Navigating the Mersey proved difficult. The channel was tortuous, the river three miles broad but riddled with sandbanks. At one point a biggish wave, similar to that which MacGregor had experienced on the Reuss (*see* p. 25), struck Harry, who was paddling the canoe, on the chest.

Approaching Ellesmere port they risked a long haul across the mud to a six-mile row. The mud proved softer and softer until it completely enveloped their legs and only some timely help from Will, who had extricated himself with the canoe, avoided a more serious rescue. Several onlookers helped them carry their boats on to the Ellesmere canal and no sooner had they washed the mud off than they were surprised to see a tug towing 14 barges. They reached Chester later that afternoon in time to stock up with mutton chops and biscuits.

The officials of the Ellesmere canal generously allowed the boats to travel toll free and kept them overnight in their warehouse without charge. Nevertheless, portaging the craft round the numerous locks was wearisome and at one the canoe's mackintosh apron was nearly lost and only retrieved by paying a boy to undress and jump in the water. Several lock-keepers kindly allowed the boats through and on reaching the branch to Wales they came upon two barges bound from Nantwich to Llangollen. One was drawn by a mule, the other by a couple of donkeys and the boatmen kindly put their boats aboard to pass the five locks ahead. It was so comfortable sitting on the roof of the cabin, that they decided to have supper and leave their boats on board overnight.

After spending the night once again all in one bed, at the *Hawk and Buckle* at Wrenbury, they had to run eight miles along the canal bank the next morning to catch up with the barges which had left at 5 a.m. As it was raining they stayed with them to the canal junction to Welshpool. Then, after carrying the boats round four locks, they paddled for a couple of hours until they came to the Perry, a small stream which forms a tributary of the Severn. Being tired of the canal, they soon floated the boats on the meandering brook and enjoyed winding about the fields and under occasional bridges. At last the river became broad enough to use the oars, and they soon reached the outskirts of Ruyton where.the *Powis Arms* could provide only one large bed for the three of them.

They covered 10 miles between 7 a.m. and 5.30 p.m. the next day, experiencing all the hazards of a wayward stream—shallows, sinuosities, overhanging branches, fallen trees, water mills and cattle fences until their rapid rivulet met the Severn. It was not until 8 p.m. that they reached Shrewsbury, 15 miles away, but here the *Wanderer* got stuck halfway across a weir and only the author's resolution in jumping into the chilly water saved her from breaking her back. Not until 9 p.m. did they reach Quarry Ferry Boathouse.

The next day the *Wanderer* was no sooner afloat than she was carried against one of the piers of Shrewsbury Bridge, forced broadside and soon filled with water. The crew were soaked but the boat remained sound. The author admits that the clumsiness was entirely his own, and advises the reader to take the accounts of a solitary traveller of his own performance 'cum grano salis', since the temptation to omit the absence of mishap is great. It is not quite clear what he means when he adds 'Boatmen, who like our friend MacGregor have learned to love their boats, will understand why I think so much of this incident and what our feelings were when straining every nerve and muscle to get free'.[26] It does, however, suggest that our author knew something more about MacGregor than the general reader!

After spending the night at the *Swan* in Ironbridge, they visited the china works at Coalport and paddled past magnificent scenery to Bewdley. The following day they reached Worcester, but not without losing their wading shoes as they shot a 50-foot rapid. A brief stop at Upton on Severn, the next night at Tewkesbury. When some four miles from Gloucester, they went ashore to allow the bore to pass. 'A great wall of water about four feet in height, extending entirely across the river, was moving swiftly up stream at the rate of six or seven miles an hour, followed by a succession of broader walls nearer and nearer together till at last the whole body of water was flowing steadily upwards.'

At Gloucester they launched their boats on the Berkeley Ship Canal and accepted a tow from a tug as far as the Stroudwater Canal. Here they found a set of five locks over 600 yards and misguidedly put their boats on an ascending barge. It took 90 minutes to cover the flight so they resolved to portage the rest, only to be confronted by a lock-keeper at Stroud demanding the full toll for passing over the Company's water, whether the locks were used or not. A lengthy discussion ensued and 'he will never know how near he was then to using the Company's water himself'.

After spending four nights with friends in Stroud, the party entered the Thames & Severn Canal on payment of 10 shillings for each boat with the option of a further pound a-piece if they wanted to use the locks. When they reached the canal company's office six locks later an official rushed out to see their pass but being in peevish mood they treated him pretty scurvily. They then hired a cart to carry the boats up the remaining 18 locks across five miles of hilly country to the Sapperton tunnel. 'Once in we could see the other end shining like the point of a pin, at a distance of two miles and a quarter. For half an hour we paddled along, as there was not sufficient water for the oars. There was no towing-path. The canal was of a uniform depth of three feet, with a sandy bottom, and as clear as crystal. When we emerged at the other end we really appeared to be floating on air, the water was so limpid that one could scarcely see it. The day was magnificent.'[27] Shortly they met

45. Sapperton Canal tunnel by candlelight, 1868. Pleasure boats continued to pass through the tunnel until about 1911. It was not legally closed until 1927

46. Hart's weir on the Upper Thames, *c.* 1860

a light pleasure boat passing towards the tunnel, with two undergraduates who had spent a week coming up from Oxford (the author referred to them as 'evidently advanced sybarites') but their encounter was of short duration as they declined the canoeists' invitation to join them for breakfast. That evening the party stopped at Cricklade Wharf and spent a pleasant night at the *White Horse*.

After three hours paddling along the Thames & Severn they put their boats on the Thames shortly before reaching the canal's junction with the river at Inglesham. This created suspicion in the tollkeeper's mind, who, having seen them on the canal, suspected them of trying to evade him and asked loudly for their pass. The crew, who were out of temper with the portaging of the locks and the abundant weed in the river, took umbrage at his manner and made the poor chap run quite a way after them before showing him their tickets.

The Thames Conservancy charged a toll of sixpence per boat per lock whether the lock was used or not so the labour of portaging the boats was now avoided. The *Wanderer*, with Harry and Will on board, shot 10 feet over Hart's weir at Kelmscott and disappeared in a cloud of spray.* Two rugs were lost but after changing their clothes at the weirside inn (the *Anchor*), they resumed their voyage only to find the local inns full, and it was not until 10 o' clock that night that they found a room. On reaching Oxford the following afternoon, they spent the following nights at Wallingford and Henley and some days later completed their voyage beneath Cannon Street Railway Bridge.

* H. W. Taunt stated that Hart's Weir had the greatest fall (over 3 feet in dry summers) of the weirs on the Upper Thames. In 1871 he recollected how one winter when there was very little fall he had scraped his face against the bridge while going under lying on his back. A boat slide was installed in 1911 but the weir was not removed until 1937.

The author concluded his account with some hints to would-be excursionists and the view that 'our trip to London, although undertaken at the close of the dry weather when we had the double disadvantage of a scarcity of water for our boats and a superabundance for ourselves was most thoroughly enjoyed throughout'.

Chapter VIII

BADEN-POWELL AND THE *NAUTILUS* (1869)

Warington Baden-Powell—his canoe cruise on the Baltic—account of voyage published in the Cornhill Magazine *(1870) and in book form (1871)—dined with John MacGregor—pleasures of canoeing—boating activities of the Baden-Powell family.*

WARINGTON BADEN-POWELL (1847–1921) was 10 years' older than his celebrated youngest brother General Sir Robert Baden-Powell, and began his career in the merchant navy with the Peninsular & Orient Line on the route to India, before going to the Bar. He practised in the Admiralty Court, the Wreck Court and on the Northern Circuit and became a Queen's Counsel. Boating was a natural development of his love of an open-air life, which did so much to influence Robert's interest in camping and scouting, and whereas MacGregor was recognised as introducing the 'Rob Roy' paddling canoe, it was Baden-Powell who popularized the sailing canoe.

Baden-Powell found two distinct pleasures in canoeing: 'one the healthful enjoyment of a free and easy life in fine weather and varied scenery, and the other, the more sensational, cracking on under sail, and working through and over heavy seas'.

In 1869 Baden-Powell and a friend named in his account only as 'H' paddled and sailed their 'Rob Roy' canoes by river, canal and lake across Sweden. The *Nautilus* and the *Isis* were shipped by steamer from Gravesend to Gothenburg, which was reached on 20 July 1869.

It was a voyage of little incident and some hardship and were it not for the useful hints on canoe travelling the book would have hardly justified publication. The reader's main impressions are of two youthful canoeists soaked to the skin, braving miserable weather for much of the six-week cruise. Drenching rain, squalls, head winds and rough water must have made MacGregor's voyages seem like luxury cruises.

Their food and accommodation was also often frugal. The second night was spent on the rocky banks of the Gotha river inside their canoes, lying on a rug in their wet clothes covered only by a mackintosh. On occasions when searching for somewhere dry to rest for the night they found no house, no sign of human life, darkness increasing and rain threatening, drizzling or pouring. When they did find accommodation, it was often no more than a barn or hay loft. Even at the *Grand Hotel* at Oxlö they could dine only on black bread-and-butter, eggs, milk and hot water, and share a large upper chamber serving as a dormitory. 'H', whoever he was, does not appear to have said a word in complaint, and it is intriguing that Warington should have made no references to his travelling companion throughout the book.

The most enjoyable feature of the cruise, if not the hardships, was the scenery. The lock flights at Trollhatten and at Berg on the East Gotha Canal, both over 120 feet, impressed them and so did the fine landscape between the Motala river and lake Glan. 'Here lofty rocks tower up on either side, stormbrands of ages on their rugged sides; masses of sombre-leaved firs tufting the crags which overhang the river, whilst in other parts the scene changes, and one glides through homely, cultivated lands, bright, grassy meadows, and English river scenery.'

The sight of their canoes aroused much local interest, but their ignorance of Swedish resulted in little dialogue with those they encountered. However, the Swedish daily *Aften Blatt* grandly announced their arrival in Stockholm in the following terms: 'The two Englishmen of whom we have spoken before, as travelling through Sweden with their canoes, have arrived in the capital, and landed on the south side of the Gustav Adolf Square. As soon as the travelling gentlemen had landed, they drew their boats out of the water, and taking them under each arm, they promenaded the city.' Modestly, the pair admitted four porters were at hand to help.

From Stockholm they took steamer to Malmo and en route visited the naval dockyard at Carlskrona where they observed two minotaurs, one of which, the *John Ericson*, they thought most remarkable as it had two heavy guns in one turret.

47. Baden-Powell sailing in the *Nautilus*, 1869

'H' and Baden-Powell, for no given reason, made the crossing from Malmo to Denmark independently. It was not an easy crossing. The weather was boisterous and it came on to blow so hard that the canoe had to be periodically baled out. After resting on the island of Saltholm and seeing numerous seals, Baden-Powell arrived in Copenhagen to find that 'H' had forestalled him and that the *Isis* was already laid up in the hall of the *Phoenix Hotel*. From here they took train and steamer to Kiel where they spied three find iron-clads of the Prussian fleet. Another train took them to Hamburg, where they stayed a week at the *Kronprinz Hotel* and sailed on the Alster. However, Baden-Powell found night cruising on the town-end of the lake

48. The *Nautilus* and the *Isis* on the Alster, Hamburg

very dangerous owing to the number of boats steaming and pulling about in all directions. The canoes were finally shipped by steamer back to London and paddled back to Searle's 'rather scratched and bumped, well seasoned with brine and sun, but still sound in wind and limb'.

The story of their exploits appeared in two issues of the *Cornhill Magazine* (October and November 1870, p. 457 *et seq*. and p. 534 *et seq*.). This account was printed in book form the following year with the title 'Canoe Travelling: log of a cruise on the Baltic', and included a long section on practical hints on building and fitting up canoes and what was now almost traditional advice on stores, clothing and cooking. Tea was recommended as being less bulky than coffee, Leibig's beef essence as useful when fish and eggs were not available, brandy to purify bad water and to drink when no beer or milk was available. Indispensable items were gold, tool chest, varnish, putty, sheath knives, fishing tackle, breach-loading pistol and a 'dark eye-glass for use when steering with the sun in front'. An Inverness cape was recommended for chilly nights and a mackintosh sheet to form a tent. The 'Rob Roy' cooker on its tripod was described as a 'little wonder', able at times to boil a quart of soup in five minutes but unruly in wind.

Baden-Powell claimed that, since MacGregor's voyage six years before, 'hundreds of canoes have been built, vast improvements made, other long foreign voyages successfully accomplished, the experiences of each, when made known, helping in the general improvement of canoes and their fittings, till, already in these few years, the first travelling canoes bear no comparison with those of the present time'.[28]

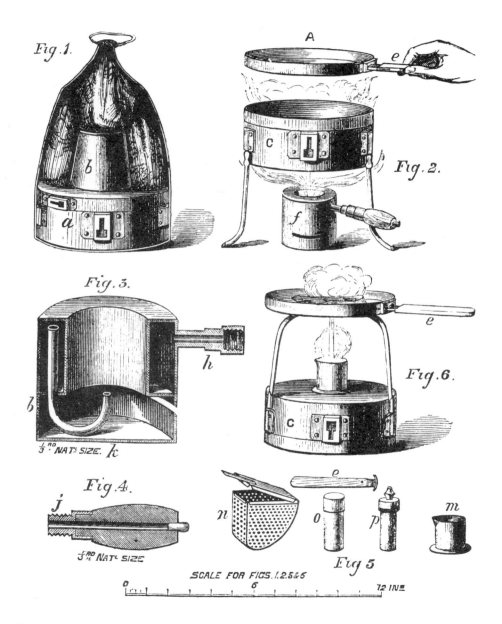

49. The 'Rob Roy' cuisine, or the 'paddler's kitchen'. It was used by MacGregor on five of his voyages and also by the British expeditionary force sent to Abyssinia to rescue the captives held by the Emperor Theodore at Magdala (1868–9)

Shortly after the book appeared in 1871, John MacGregor briefly recorded in his diary that on 20 December he met Browning the poet and 'dined B. Powell'. MacGregor was 22 years older than Warington Baden-Powell and one can only speculate on how the two men got on. Baden-Powell found himself differing with MacGregor in one respect. He wrote 'To some men there is an intense enjoyment in being alone with their thoughts in a foreign country for months together, the spell only to be broken at intervals by the necessary intercourse with the natives. I have enjoyed many a short solitary cruise, solitary because mine was the only canoe in those parts of the world, but on a long trip I should prefer as many companions as possible, for even when two are together every trouble is halved and pleasure doubled.'[29] And yet on his voyage to the Baltic there is not a single mention of any singular incident or conversation with his companion 'H'.

The year following his return from the Baltic, the Baden-Powell family decided to spend the summer holidays in the Wye valley. Warington, together with his brothers George and Robert (now aged 15), paddled their canoes up the Thames 'till the river became a stream and finally a brook that was too small to float us'; then carted their craft to the upper waters of the Avon. After paddling, sailing, poling or towing downstream to Bath, Bristol and Avonmouth, they voyaged along the left bank of the Severn, crossed the river to Chepstow and northwards along the Wye into Wales.[30]

The closing lines of Baden-Powell's log refer to the *Nautilus* being overhauled preparatory to a cruise in the Mediterranean, but no confirmation of this trip has been found. The author married late in life in 1913. He also wrote *Sea Scouting for Boys* which Robert, then Lord Baden-Powell, revised in 1931, mentioning his debt to his elder brother for his early guidance in scouting. *Canoe Travelling* was not reprinted, but Baden-Powell did contribute the 10-page article on canoeing for the 1897 edition of Suffolk's *Encyclopaedia of Sport and Games*. In this he wrote 'The 'Rob Roy' type is well enough on easy rivers, canals, ditches and such like; but in a really bad rapid and for rough portaging, she is a poor craft. The camp kit and clothes that can be stowed in canoes of the Rob Roy type are about fit for a doll, certainly not reasonable for a man, unless an hotel is more or less a certainty every night.'[31] How MacGregor would have protested at this slight, but by now he, alas, was dead.

Chapter IX

JAMES MOLLOY'S AUTUMN HOLIDAY
ON FRENCH RIVERS (1873)

James Molloy, sportsman, barrister and composer—holiday plans—forming a crew—departure from Caudebec—the Marie *swamped—rescued from the Seine—a week at Rouen—further adversities—stuck in the mud—Poissy and Paris and the Haute Seine—Canal du Loing and d'Orleans closed for repair—a 60-mile walk with a wagon for the* Marie—*down the Loire from Orleans to Nantes—dangerous quicksands—St Florent—up the Breton Canal to Redon.*

BY THE EARLY 1870s boating excursions 'had', according to Mansfield, 'become so popular that scarcely a year passes without one or more boats being conveyed across the Channel to investigate the Continental streams'.[31a] One of these was by James Molloy (1837–1909) and his crew. He was an Irishman educated at the Catholic university of Dublin who continued his studies at London University, Paris and Bonn. He was called to the Bar in 1863 and joined the south-eastern circuit but did not practise. Already he was becoming something of a song writer and during the period from 1865 to 1900 he composed nearly one hundred, many of which were popular.

A keen sportsman and in early life an athlete, Molloy's account of the rowing exploits of his colleagues and himself on the Seine and the Loire was the first narrative to dwell on the humorous side of boating. His predecessors had rather too faithfully logged the details and omitted the fun, and it is Molloy to whom both Stevenson and Jerome owe a debt. Even so, the story of his holiday adventure occupies 51 chapters and, although full of incident, there are unnecessary digressions and it could with advantage have been shortened. The charm of the book is enhanced by the drawings of Linley Sambourne (1844–1910), the cartoonist and illustrator who had only recently joined the staff of *Punch* and who was to become well known for his illustrations of Charles Kingsley's *Water Babies*.

Molloy was a man acutely sensitive to his surroundings. He had an ear for sound —the murmuring of streams, the movement of cattle, the music of church bells. He had an eye for beauty; he would find poetry in the bricks of a lime kiln or a cobbled street. 'Al fresco' lunches would be eaten amidst fine landscapes. He was good at observation and interested in people. He wrote that he could only look and wonder, as the sun set and twilight fell, at the beauty of the river, 'at the hues and tints we had never before seen—at the majesty of the shadows coming up so suddenly—at the stars one after another glistening deep in the water'.[32] Above all, it was the 'very tranquility of the little stream and its unknown villages was not an unpleasing change from the rush of the great rivers and their big cities'.[33]

In traditional style, the author concludes his tale with the hope that the reminiscences of their holiday 'may be found worthy of repetition by those who have health, strength, and experience to appreciate a trip beyond all telling the most enjoyable'.

The first chapter begins like a play with stage directions and the scene 'A room in the Temple overlooking the river'. It is evening following a day of intense heat. It is near the end of the season and a few men just up from the circuit have dropped in to discuss projects for the long vacation. Some are for the moors, others the Med. Ashantee is talked of and some propose a steam yacht for a cruise on the Belgian canals. The scene changes as they troop off through the Temple Gardens to Searle's boathouse where they jump into a four and go for a spin on the river. The idea of a holiday afloat is aired and within a few days a crew of four formed. The names of two of the crew, known as Two and Three, are not revealed; Linley Sambourne is referred to as 'Bow'; the author as 'Stroke'. Only the coxswain's place waits to be filled. 'He had his own maps and guide books, and in fact we ran up little bills for him on all sides. But we only knew him as 20 per cent of the expenses, and put him down in the list as X—and certainly there never was a more unknown quantity.'[34] Indeed, his seat was never permanently taken.

Much of the humour foreshadows that of Jerome K. Jerome. In many instances it is certainly as amusing. For instance, it was agreed to carry in the boat 'nothing but the absolute change that was necessary and send on the luggage from town to town. There was the most pleasing unanimity on the point till we came to examine our things on the eve of departure when the accumulation of pet luxuries would have swamped a much larger craft!' Sambourne himself produced two dressing bags, a portable armchair for sketching, a sunshade and a portmanteau. Two pages later we learn about the dog, Gyp, a black and tan, belonging to Sambourne. 'His passion for stones was ruining his teeth, and undermining his constitution. It was often embarrassing to the crew, for, under some sudden inspiration, he would take a header from the boat in one of his diving fits, and nothing but getting out, and wading or swimming after him (which he gloried in) would induce him to come back.'

Straw hats and jerseys had been ordered in Bond Street, blue and white outfits from Savile Row. Messenger of Teddington were asked to provide a new four-oared 40-foot outrigger and ship it to Le Havre. Here the crew assembled, but rough water in the estuary prompted the crew to put the *Marie* on board a steamer up to Caudebec, where the night was spent at the *Aigle d'Or*. Like so many boating tales, no sooner had they left Caudebec than thick clouds gathered. Not a summer shower but a steadily determined downpour. The tide was dead against, the water low and only mud banks to be seen. Five, 10, 12 miles, and then the rain stopped and the crew paddled on to Duclair where the only accommodation available was two tiny rooms in an auberge.

After an enjoyable evening the crew rowed with the tide towards Rouen. However, on entering one of the long eight-mile reaches of the Seine whose width here was nearly ¾ mile, they found the wind coming directly at them in treacherous squalls. Every now and then a wave would hiss along the gunwale and before long the boat was labouring heavily. Suddenly, a larger wave swept over Linley Sambourne, the *Marie* was swamped and the crew, oars, dressing bags, boots and jackets were floating in the middle of the river. The artist attempted to swim for shore but, after striking out bravely, he became weighed down by his boots and heavy woollen Guernsey and only returned with difficulty. The boat floated keel upwards; the crew clung to the boat. There was no-one in sight and no help at hand.

And then by the merest chance three quarters of an hour later the ferryman from the Ile St Georges appeared, rescued them, the boat and some of their belongings. Almost everything valuable had sunk. They had also lost the rudder of the *Marie*, so they abandoned her and set off on foot. Their path shortly led them to a cottage inn whose landlord showed not the slightest surprise at their condition and gave them coffee, eggs and excellent cognac. They walked on through the forest of Roumere to Rouen. Finding lodgings at the *Hotel d'Angleterre*, its hospitality was greatly praised. The hotel staff rallied round to get their clothes dry in time for dinner and they passed a pleasant evening. The next day they returned to the *Marie* and rowed up to Rouen in spite of their lost rudder, but with the assistance of an elderly 'cox'.

Molloy's first impression of Rouen is of the *Hotel d'Angleterre*, in front of which 'was a little garden of white marble tables, shady plants, and comfortable causeuses. A long promenade screened from the road and the river by a row of trees. Some way down, streams of light shone in the shop windows. At the end of the promenade a large and very bright café. The people sat under the trees, or walked up and down. Pretty dresses, and cavalry uniforms glancing by. Beyond rose the tall masts and rigging of the vessels at anchor.'[35]

After spending a week or more at Rouen and a Norman chateau, awaiting the replacement of their lost baggage, they set off once more only to be nearly swamped by a combination of wind and tide within the first mile and so were forced to make port and forward the *Marie* 80 miles by boat to the sleepy village of Vernon while the crew took the train. Here they saw a little shop, 'Rive, Fabricant de Parapluies'. There was no-one inside and only one very blue, very old and very unsatisfactory looking umbrella in the window. A few hens were asleep on the counter!

After visiting Grand Andelys, they walked the following day to Mantes. Two days later the tug towing the train of barges appeared with the *Marie* on board, but as the captain would not stop to unload, the crew had to join the barge train. As dusk was falling the barges went aground so the party had to return to Mantes for the night. The following day they succeeded in launching the *Marie* and, with a little boy as cox, rowed in pouring rain up to the lock at Meulan. Avoiding the main stream where possible, they rowed up the backwaters to Poissy, the great cattle market of Paris, and that night went to a big fête held in the heart of the forest of St Germain.

Molloy observed, on passing the junction of the Seine and the Oise, that it was a 'bright joyous looking spot dotted with solemn old barges that came down from Holland, and the bright red caps of the Dutch sailors. We looked with longing at this new river that would have taken us by Pontoise, Beaumont, Compiegne and La Fere to the Ardennes, but shot on, leaving for another year so pleasant a trip'.*

Landing at Pecq, they decided to run up by train to Paris for the night at *Meurice's Hotel*. On returning to Pecq they found a new cox, Jean Bouroon, former servant of 'Three', who proved 'invaluable in difficulties' and was a bright cheery companion.

---

* The route taken by Moens and, in the reverse direction, by R. L. Stevenson and Sir Walter Simpson (*see* Chapters X and XI).

50. The crew of the *Marie* voyaging up the Seine on a river chaumière

They avoided the lock at Bougival by carrying the boat across the island, and spent the night at Asnières where the *Marie* was abandoned for a week while the crew went their own way. The boat was then brought up to Grenelle. The journey through Paris was slow and tedious and there was added frustration when no accommodation could be found in Choisy-le-Roi.

Beyond Paris at the lock near Ivry they met a French crew going on a similar cruise through the Nivernais canals in a boat which was like a small barge with a roomy deck cabin. They decided to join the Frenchmen who were being towed up river behind a string of barges. Two days later they arrived at Melun, by which time Molloy's injured hand was on the mend. A delightful pull to St Mamès, where they hoped to join the Canals du Loing and Orleans for 90 miles to reach the Loire above Orleans, but in this they were disappointed for the waterways were under repair and closed for six weeks. And so there was nothing for it but a wagon for the *Marie* and a 60-mile tramp across country to Orleans.

Except for spending a couple of days in Fontainebleau, noticing chalked slogans reading 'Vive Napoleon IV' and enjoying a superb paté d'alouettes at Pithiviers, the walk was uneventful. Launching the *Marie* on the waters of the Loire exactly one month after their departure from Le Havre, they began to row downstream. The surrounding country had a very desolate appearance as they paddled through wastes of sand, striking the odd sandbank. A brief stop at Les Mauves and then, continuing

51. Stuck on a Loire sandbank

to sweep past the intricate sand islands, they spent the night at Beaugency. 'Our arrival was quite a little excitement for the old town. One of the crew in one street, another in the next, and so on, each the centre of a group of men and women who were prepared to ask questions and go on chatting all night.'

The next day they rowed to Blois and went to a performance of Offenbach's *Le Violineux*. Continuing down the Loire, they stopped at Chaumont to sketch the chateau and spent the night at Amboise where they had to shoot the blocked arches of the bridge—'there was one opening, and one only, a narrow streak of water that dropped suddenly a foot half-way under the bridge. It was a water-fence and half the boat's length must have been in the air as she went over'.

At Tours (where they at last caught up with the fifth man) they found they attracted little interest, but enjoyed an evening at the Café Chantant. It was beyond Tours that they now came upon the dangerous quicksands where only a few days before their arrival six young men had gone bathing and, crossing what they supposed was a sandbank, had been drawn down and engulfed. To find, and keep to the barge channel, was not easy. Although marked by lines of thin stakes, the winding channel was so narrow, the current so strong, that it was difficult not to flatten them with the *Marie's* length. Near Lugnes they were rowing hard, when they struck something and while Stroke was trying to rejoin the boat which had been swept downstream, he and 'Two' sank up to their knees on what they thought was dry sand. Fortunately, the two who remained on board were able to row back to pick them up from what was the edge of a shifting quicksand.

They arrived at Langeais in the midst of a village fête, in which they at once participated. Beyond St Patrice the Loire began widening out and the enormous wastes of sand soon disappeared after the junction with the Vienne where the river was a mile or more broad.

While staying at Saumur they drove out to see the dolmens of Begneux. Beside this rude temple stood the dolmen-keeper's cottage in which the crew wrote their names in the visitors' book.

The fine scenery around Gennes and Les Rosiers and the panoramic splendour of Ponts de Cé, where the Maine joined the Loire, made the 40-mile row to Angers most enjoyable. However, the last seven miles up the Maine, where they moored for the night by the floating laundry, was a hard pull. Returning to Ponts de Cé they lunched some miles downstream in the boat in the shadow of two deserted windmills before reaching the ruins of the Chateau de Chantocé. About Montrelais the sandbanks became troublesome but after landing at the 'loveliest spot we had yet seen', the village of St Florent—the scene of the rising of the Le Vendée rebellion

52. Lunching on the Loire above Chalonnes

of 1793—they found a charming inn for the night. Indeed, after rowing on to Nantes some 40 miles away, the crew returned by train to the village for some fishing and a three-day stay.

After a night at Nantes and the departure of number 'Five', they passed through the lock to the Erdre and set out on their northward journey by the Breton Canal to Dinan and St Malo. They joined the Canal du Brest at the lock de Quilheix and, finding no accommodation en route, they pressed on by night to Blain. Suddenly, in pitch darkness they hit the stone wall of a lock (La Remandais) and stove in the bows. A long walk through the meadows brought them to a village inn where they spent the night; it was also the only shop whose variety of merchandise included bacon, boots, mustard, whipcord and hats.

After repairing the boat, they rowed through a wild and lovely countryside. The picturesque lockhouses had verandahs covered with grapes. They saw the remaining tower (formerly there were nine) of the ruined Chateau de Blain. The only barges seen on the canal lay at anchor in the bay by the old bridge. The crew had intended

53. The Chateau de Blain between Nantes and Redon. The 14th-century castle has been
partially restored

54. Title page to the first edition of *Our Autumn Holiday on French Rivers* drawn by
Linley Sambourne

reaching St Malo via Dinan and the river Rance but both 'Bow' and 'Three' had insufficient time to spare, so they took the *Marie* by train from Redon to St Malo.

The voyage thus concluded, Molloy commented that 'from the first to the last stroke of the cruise, the interest went on increasing no matter where we were; and two months more of such wanderings would have been gladly welcomed'.

The first edition of *Our Autumn Holiday on French Rivers* is attractively bound in green or brown gilt-decorated cloth with the crew of the *Marie* and the dog Gyp depicted in their straw boaters on the front cover. W.H.G.F. refers to it in the *Dictionary of National Biography* as a 'charmingly written prose work'. It was republished in a cheap edition in 1879.

In the same year as his 'autumn holiday', Molloy published an edition of Irish tunes entitled *Songs of Ireland*. The following year he married Florence, the youngest daughter of Henry Baskerville of Crowsley Park, Henley-on-Thames. Later in life Molloy acted as secretary to the attorney-general and resided in London. In 1889 he was made private chamberlain to Pope Leo XIII. He died in 1909.

There is no doubt that the account of his holiday on French rivers is amusingly written and that its moderate success was equally due to the fine illustrations by Linley Sambourne. Balfour claims in his two-volume *Life of Stevenson* that it was Molloy's voyage which suggested his own expedition,[36] but similar claims can be made for the exploits of Hamerton, MacGregor and Moens.

Chapter X

WILLIAM MOENS AND THE STEAM YACHT *YTENE* (1875)

His early life—captured by brigands in Italy (1865)—sails his steam yacht to Strasburg (1869)—describes his voyage in the Ytene to Paris (1875)—the river Oise to Compiègne— St Quentin canal—Tronquay tunnel—a coal barge nearly sinks—via the Scheldt into Belgium— Condé—Mons—public interest in the yacht—the Willebroek canal to Brussels—Moens has a mishap—Ghent—Bruges—Ostend—Canal de Calais—return via Dover Harbour to Lymington— book published (1876).

55. William Moens

WILLIAM MOENS (1833–1904) was the son of a Dutch merchant who had emigrated to England early in the 19th century. Moens began his career on the Stock Exchange, but soon retired to Hampshire where he spent much of his time yachting and later in antiquarian research, studying forest law and local government. He was one of the founders of the Huguenot Society of London (1885), deeply interested in the New Forest, a magistrate and a member of Hampshire County Council.

In 1863 he had married Anne Warlters and in January 1865 he travelled with her to Sicily and Naples. While returning with friends from photographing the temples at Paestum, he and the Rev. John Aynsley were captured by a band of brigands. Aynsley was released the next day with a ransom note for £8000. Moens remained a prisoner for four months. He was insufficiently clad and often starving, forced frequently to sleep in caves and scramble across rugged mountainous country, while Italian soldiers harried the band from a distance. Strenuous efforts were made by his wife and friends for his release and eventually he was freed on payment of £5100. Moens wrote a lively two-volume account of this episode in *English Travellers and Italian Brigands*.

In 1869 he sailed his steam yacht *Cicada* from Lymington up the Rhine to Strasburg, and by the French canals to Paris and Le Havre passing 219 locks and five tunnels. Moens recalled that his voyage was regarded with great interest in France, as no steamers had successfully traversed the route before, although two steam barges had failed in the attempt.[37] Although he apparently kept a detailed log of this trip—he recorded the fact that he passed the 2½-mile Mauvages tunnel in 37 minutes[38]—it was not published.

It was therefore perhaps a trifle surprising that he should decide to publish his account of a similar voyage six years later. There is no doubt he was a man who loved detail. Besides descriptions of visits to places of historical, ecclesiastical and industrial interest, Moens itemizes the amount of coal burnt, oil used, canal dues, pilots' fees, the price of beet and even the price of peaches. As one of the barge-masters who met Robert Louis Stevenson reported, 'He came ashore at all the locks and asked the names of the villages, whether from boatmen or lock-keepers; and then he wrote them down. O he wrote enormously! I suppose it was a wager'. An original reason for taking notes, thought R.L.S.[39]

Moens wrote his account for the enjoyment and pleasure of others, that they might be aware of 'a new mode of travel whereby a party may by the aid of steam luxuriously pass through a great part of Europe carrying their hotels with them and enjoy most of the pleasures of yachting'. The decision to voyage through France and Belgium was made more or less on the spur of the moment. August 1875 was nearly gone and the weather threatening when Moens, his 42nd birthday just celebrated, found himself cruising around Fowey in his 45-ton steam yacht *Ytene*, wondering what to do. Meeting the owner of another steamer, a trip through France was suggested and as is the habit of the rich, 'our minds were soon made up to go to Paris and explore the north of France and Belgium'.

The *Ytene* was a 72½-foot vessel with a 11 ft. 3 ins. beam and a draught of 4 ft. 8 ins. (1.42 metres). She had 20 h.p. engines which could produce 14 knots, consumed 75 lbs of coal an hour on inland waters and from 112 to 168 lbs while at sea, but her bunkers could hold only four tons. And so on 28 August Moens steamed the *Ytene* for the Solent to lay in a store of provisions, ship lightweight collapsible masts, clean the boilers and fill the bunkers. Additional sacks of coal were stacked on deck for the passage to Le Havre.

The crew consisted of Moens as captain and chief engineer; Fisher, engineer and stoker; Miller, the mate, who was in charge of cabin duties, and Allen the boy cook. Guests were 'received' on board from time to time and taken on excursions, but little mention is made of them or of his wife Anne. Sadly her name which appears in print abbreviated as 'A———' occurs only three times in the book while details of lengths and widths and distances, and the suppliers' quality and price of beetroot and steam coal are regularly provided. There were also on board two black-and-tan toy terriers, 'Titus' and 'Lill', who took little part in the events to be narrated.

The voyage across the Channel by night was uneventful, and little of interest is recorded on the journey up the Seine except the need for pilots, due to the hazards in passing the bridges destroyed during the Franco-Prussian War (1870–1). At Rouen they hired Rousillon, a retired chief pilot, 'a quiet obliging man who kept a wine shop and billiard table at 20 Quai de Paris'. Watching the haymakers at St Oissel twist the dry grass into small bundles reminded Moens of his experiences of Italian mountain life 10 years before.

A couple of days were spent admiring the beauties of Les Andelys, where Moens brought out his photographic apparatus. One day was spent photographing the castle: 'It was intensely hot below but a nice breeze tempered the sultry air and enabled us to spend the day in comfort, though the labour of walking about to find the right points of view, and to expose the plates was great. Luncheon was sent up

56. The steam yacht *Ytene* on the Seine, 1874

to us from the yacht below, and when I had taken six views and packed up the apparatus, we sat down and enjoyed the prospect.' At La Roche Guyon they found the London steamer *Arion* bound for Paris, stopped and unloading cargo into barges as the water level had fallen too low—she was drawing five feet. At Guernes they noticed many washerwomen and donkeys carrying the washing to town. After a brief stop at Mantes, they moored for the night above Meulan and reached Paris the next day where they berthed opposite the Tuileries gardens.

After spending nearly a fortnight in Paris visiting among other things the Maritime Exhibition in the Champs Elysées and the Geographical Exhibition in the

Louvre, and during which Fisher, who was a great tram traveller but knew no French, found himself at the wrong end of a terminus and had an unpleasant night out, they steamed down the Seine past Bougival to the river Oise.

Five miles up the Oise they observed Chateau Vauréal; then passing between Evangy and Pontoise, they proceeded past Champagne and Royaument. 'All the barges met were coal-laden coming from the Belgian coalfields; they were very deep having 270 tons on board and drawing six feet of water.'

Moens is keenly interested in all he sees, noting a nail factory, a sugar refinery, stone quarries, iron-works, as well as discoursing on churches and buildings of historic interest. Passing under triple-arched Port St Maxence, built in 1774, he comments that this was one of Perronet's best works. They saw the pleasure boats on the lakes of the Palace at Compiègne used in the time of the Emperor. 'Merry and gay was the forest then; parties and sports of every kind made it ring with joy and laughter, all of which the poor residents in the forest villages now look on as things of the past, and not likely to return except with a return of the Empire.'

The visit to Compiègne was a success (except for the theft of a rubber deck sheet by a bargee) and, leaving there on 27 September with a strong wind blowing behind them, they passed Jonville and Chauny locks, which were so crowded that they were stowed fender to fender with the barges. They procured a carriage to view the dungeons of Courcy but were refused permission to view the glass works at Chauny by the managing director, Monsieur Bivet, who was really most 'uncivil'. Moens trusted that 'he when visiting England will never meet with the reception that he gave an English gentleman and lady who wished to see foreign industries'. The factory employed some 2000 hands working in shifts day and night and the nearby chemical works another 1500. Moens couldn't resist adding 'we heard that the workmen suffer much in their health in these works, many losing all their teeth'.

The following day they passed 10 or so locks on the St Quentin canal, noting the tramways to the coal mines near Voyaux, that the people in this part were poorer and the houses more wretched in appearance. After passing the junction to La Fère, commercial traffic diminished. At St Quentin, Moens noticed that a baker was delivering bread in his cart and still using for each house a wooden tally on which a notch was cut for each loaf.

Two hours after leaving St Quentin they passed through Tronquay tunnel whose centre height (17 feet) was just two feet higher than their funnel. On the other side they were forced to lie up behind a line of barges stretching at least 1000 yards which were being towed by a submerged chain. Ahead lay the long tunnel of Riqueval, and further delay ensued when the line heaved-to to allow a long string of barges coming in the opposite direction to pass. Moens decided to overtake the 30 or so barges ahead of him and so be the first to enter the 3½-mile tunnel. No sooner was this accomplished than at about 9 p.m. they heard a great outcry as men hastily explained that one of the oncoming barges heavily laden with coal was sinking in the tunnel. 'This was a pretty state of things, and we soon thought that our route to Belgium would be barred for weeks, and that we might have to retrace our way back again.' The tug steamer soon, however, emerged from the arch, and came to a standstill when three or four barges were out of the tunnel. It was the first that was damaged, and she was already sunk in the water to within three or four inches of the gunwale.

Anne Moens did her best to comfort the crying women and children who huddled on the bank of the canal, reacting to the sight of the sinking barge as would any family seeing its home about to perish. However, the pumps gradually began to gain on the water, the hole was revealed in the starboard side and Moens contributed cotton waste to the task of patching it.

It took 70 minutes for the *Ytene* to pass through Riqueval tunnel, and then they had to pass 15 locks 'and had an altercation or two with the masters of barges who wanted us to wait for them to pass the locks first. This would never have done and in some cases I had the gates shut, and the locks filled with water, without the barge below taking its turn.' Cambrai was reached well after nightfall. Here they entered the Scheldt Navigation and, close by the lock at Selles, Moens discovered a bric-à-brac shop where nothing was priced, but where eventually he was able to purchase 'one of the real old silver tops of the velvet bags in use quite two hundred years ago and now again come into fashion; also an early edition of Télémaque and La Fontaine's *Fables*'.

From the junction with the Canal de la Sensée they passed Malin, Meuville, the iron works and brick-fields between Trith and Valenciennes; at this latter place the canal passed right through the fortifications of the citadel built by Vauban in 1621. The stronghold of Condé was considered among the most remarkable in France with 'quaint-looking' double drawbridges at all the town gates. A sentinel on guard told Moens that 'there were only two hundred soldiers and two troops of cavalry in the place'. Could it be that such facile intelligence gathering made the French more spy conscious as Hamerton and Pennell were later to discover? (*see* Chapter XII.)

After coaling, visiting the barge-building yards and spending a day exploring Condé, the *Ytene* ascended the Hayne, passing Thivencelle lock and later two cafés which marked the Belgian frontier. Beyond Herbière barges lined both banks, the descending ones laden with coal being towed by men, women and even children.

The sight of a steam yacht had caused a certain amount of interest in France and on one occasion 'two man-servants came running in haste to see us steam by', and later the news that a yacht flying English colours was alongside the quay at Compiègne aroused great excitement. Apparently the vessel created rather more interest in Belgium since theirs was the first steamer ever seen in these parts and 'we were most amused to see the way all work was suspended at the coal wharfs, and even some hundreds of yards inland, all running as hard as they could to the bank to see the unusual sight'. The locks were crowded with sightseers in some places and 'we were considered so well worth looking at that a young woman rushed out of one house with nothing but a short linen garment on, thrown very loosely round her shoulders, holding up her gown that she had hurriedly snatched up to her neck'.[40] And by the time the *Ytene* had reached Antoing, the canal engineer had even read in the paper about their travels.[41]

It took 10 days to reach Mons from Paris (210 miles) which was good going in view of the numerous locks, considerable barge traffic and stops for sight-seeing.

Two days later they steamed into the Canal d'Antoing, but on arriving at the entrance to the Blaton & Ath Canal they were delayed 12 hours by the need to obtain a special authorisation from the Department of Public Works for a steam vessel to proceed under steam. A further delay ensued when a Dutch barge refused to allow the *Ytene* to overtake, until the Dutchman went aground.

After staying a day at Ath, they passed through Lessines where the river Dendre was very narrow and the houses built up from the edge of the water. Acren, Grammont, Grimmingen, Port Santbergen and Alost were among the towns now skirted before they came upon two railway bridges which had to be swung before the yacht could pass. At Termonde they had to wait for another railway bridge to be opened before they could join the tidal Scheldt which here was some 150 yards wide. Above Tamine they observed an old twin-funnelled Ostend mail-boat, now used to sound the channel from Antwerp to Ghent, before negotiating another large railway bridge whose piers caused quite an obstruction. At Rupelmonde, where they noticed the huge brick kilns and the recently erected statue of Mercator, they turned up the Rupel river to Boom and then took the Willebroek canal to Brussels. Early on the morning of 13 October they saw one of the London to Brussels steamers pass carrying iron girders; after observing two large country seats and crossing an aqueduct over a river, they steamed into Brussels where they found three large basins; the first was used by the largest vessels, the second was where barges discharged firewood and the third was filled with barges unloading bricks, tiles and coal, and where at the extreme end they were able to berth the *Ytene* close to St Catherine's church and the general post office. Here Moens had a nasty accident. He was going ashore to get the day's *Times* when the gangplank slipped from the quay and he was flung into the water, which was 'uncommonly' cold. Able to reboard the yacht while the crew held the end of the plank, he was none the worse for his mishap.

After spending a pleasant week in Brussels, they sailed back to Termonde and on down the Scheldt past the gunpowder works of Wetteren and the tanneries of Quarterecht to Ghent. In the docks they saw Baron Rothschild's 150-ton steam yacht moored as well as 'large square rigged sea-going vessels and two English steamers unloading coals'. After a day's sight-seeing, the *Ytene* left Ghent on 21 October for Bruges. En route they met a horsedrawn 'trekschuyt', an old-fashioned passenger-carrying boat fitted with windows fore and aft and with a raised deck; country girls in provincial dress gazed from the cabins and a man at the helm blew a trumpet in salutation as they passed.

From Bruges they explored the canals between Ostend and Calais and at Nieuport Moens spied a rare pair of old Lowestoft jugs in the window of a shop which was frustratingly shut. After difficulties with weeds and shallows which meant Allen going ashore with a towline, they reached Furnes, and then at Edinkirke they had to wait for a temporary wooden bridge to be dismantled. Reaching Dunkirk, they passed through a low arch in the walls of the fortifications before steaming on to the river Aa. Soon after reaching the Canal de Calais, they came upon the remarkable Pont de Quatre Branches ou Sans Pareil, beautifully constructed in stone with a spherical vault pierced with lunettes, which was constructed in 1752 where four canals and four roads meet. Delayed a couple of days at Calais by unsettled weather they crossed the Channel to Dover where they were again forced to shelter. Then after a night in Newhaven Harbour, they finally tied up at Lymington on 1 November having steamed 1115 miles in two months, burnt 15 tons of coal and used 13½ gallons of oil.

A rich man's quite eventful voyage had been accomplished with little of the wealth of human experience which Stevenson was to encounter when making a similar journey the following year. Moens entitled his narrative *Through France and Belgium, by River and Canal in the Steam Yacht 'Ytene'*.* It was published by Hurst & Blackett of Great Marlborough Street in the summer of 1876 but was never reprinted.

---

* Hamerton refers in the *Saone, A Summer Voyage* (p. 172) to the log of the *Princess*, another English steam yacht which took five days to pass the Burgundy Canal in 1880.

Chapter XI

ROBERT LOUIS STEVENSON
AND AN INLAND VOYAGE (1876)

'I whose diminutive design,
Of sweeter cedar, pithier pine,
Is fashioned on so frail a mould,
A hand may launch, a hand withhold.
I rather with the leaping trout,
Wind, among lilies, in and out;
I the unnamed, inviolate,
Green, rustic rivers, navigate,
My dipping paddle scarcely shakes
The berry in the bramble-brakes;
Still forth on my green way I wend
Beside the cottage garden-end;
And by the nested angler fare,
And take the lovers unaware.
(The Canoe Speaks—Underwoods III)

Stevenson's love of sailing and canoeing—pleasure not the sole object of the voyage—its highlights—Antwerp Docks—Boom-Willebroek Canal—Royal Sport Nautique Laeken—train to Maubeuge—Pont sur Sambre—Landrecies—R.L.S. inspects a barge on the Sambre & Oise—capsizes—Origny—Down the Oise to Moy—La Fère of cursed memory—Noyon—Compiègne, Précy and the marionettes—Pontoise—publication of An Inland Voyage (1878)*—reasons for its popularity—J. A. Hammerton's bicycle tour (1904)—destruction of landmarks—The Eleven Thousand Virgins of Cologne.*

GRAHAM BALFOUR, Stevenson's biographer, records that the idea of the boating expedition seems to have been suggested by the publication in 1874 of Molloy's *Our Autumn Holiday on French Rivers* (*see* Chapter X), but Stevenson's familiarity with MacGregor, Hamerton and Moens indicates that he only awaited the opportunity to combine boating with writing a book. It seems likely, however, that the route taken in *An Inland Voyage* was influenced by Moens and that R.L.S. enjoyed the irony of writing about the experiences of poor travellers in the humblest craft paddling along in the reverse direction of Moen's luxurious steam yacht voyage from Paris to Boom. Stevenson's original plan was to canoe to Paris and Grez and complete their cruise next spring ('if we're all alive and jolly') by Loing and Loire, Saone and Rhône to the Mediterranean.[42] He was 26 years of age and in good health.

The cruise proved rather a cheerless experience as those who go boating in Northern Europe have often discovered. However, Stevenson was not the first man to endure the hardships of foreign travel with the object of making a book out of it and some 'coin'. Ten days after their departure, he wrote from Compiègne 'We have had deplorable weather quite steady ever since the start; not one day without heavy showers; and generally much wind and cold wind . . . I must say it has sometimes required a stout heart; and sometimes one could not help sympathising inwardly with the French folk who hold up their hands in astonishment over our pleasure journey. Indeed I do not know that I would have stuck to it as I have done, if it had not been for professional purposes; for an easy book may be written and sold, with might little brains about it, where the journey is of a certain seriousness and can be named. I mean, a book about a journey from York to London must be clever; a book about the Caucasus may be what you will. Now I mean to make this journey at least a curious one; it won't be finished these vacations.'[43]

Stevenson's favourite recreations had been walking in the forest of Fontainebleau and paddling up and down the Loing. 'The course of its pellucid river, whether up or down, is full of attractions for the navigator; the mirrored and inverted images of trees, lilies and mills, and the foam and thunder of weirs.'[44]

His companion for the voyage through Belgium and France was Sir Walter Simpson, with whom he had already shared many boating experiences on the Firth of Forth and at Grez where his cousin Bob Stevenson had devised a leather canoe of his own 'with a niche for everything' and, as his friends said, 'a place for nothing'.

Stevenson found difficulty in completing the book. Writing to Sir Sidney Colvin from Dieppe on New Year's Day 1878 'I am at the Inland Voyage again . . . I only hope (Kegan) Paul may take the thing; I want coin so badly and besides it would be something done.' However, the book appeared the following May. The reviews were generally favourable. The sales, however, were small and only in 1883 was a second edition issued. Stevenson's comment on Walter Crane's sketch for the frontispiece was that it should be a river, not a canal, and 'the look should be cruel, lewd and kindly all at once'.

The story of the inland voyage is of a canoe trip from Antwerp to within 50 miles of Paris. The country through which he and Walter Simpson passed is relatively uninteresting. Frank Swinnerton judged the book a picturesque work of travel and topography,[45] but this it is not. As an account of the places Stevenson visited it is far from complete and in any case it was not intended as a substitute for Baedeker. For when all has been said, it is not the places but the happenings and the consequences which the reader finds of greater interest. Unlike his contemporaries, his descriptions of the type of canoes used were of the briefest order—one was of cedar and the other of oak. Equally, Stevenson does not, like Moens, supply us with details of preparations or dates. In fact, the voyage began in August 1876 when 'We made a great stir in Antwerp Docks' as the two canoes, the *Arethusa* and the *Cigarette*, went off in a 'splash and a bubble of small breaking water' along the Scheldt. 'The sun shone brightly; the tide was making—four jolly miles an hour; the wind blew steadily, with occasional squalls.

'It was agreeable upon the river. A barge or two went past laden with hay. Reeds and willows bordered the stream; and cattle and grey venerable horses came and hung their mild heads over the embankment. Here and there was a pleasant village among trees, with a noisy shipping yard; here and there a villa in a lawn.'

And so up the Scheldt and the Rupel past the smoky brickyards of Boom. 'Boom is not a nice place', and Stevenson found the *Hotel de la Navigation* its worst feature.

57. R. L. Stevenson at the age of 26

'It boasts of a sanded parlour, with a bar at one end, looking on the street; another sanded parlour, darker and colder, with an empty birdcage and tricolour subscription box by way of sole adornment, where we made shift to dine in the company of three uncommunicative engineer apprentices and a silent bagman. The food, as usual in Belgium, was of a nondescript occasional character.'

Next morning in heavy and chill rain they set forth on the busy Willebroek Canal. 'Every now and then we met or overtook a long string of boats, with great green tillers; high sterns with a window on either side of the rudder, and perhaps a jug or a flowerpot in one of the windows; a dinghy following behind; a woman busied about the day's dinner, and a handful of children. These barges were all tied one behind the other with tow ropes, to the number of 25 or 30; and the line was headed and kept in motion by a steamer of strange construction. It had neither paddlewheel nor screw; but by some gear not rightly comprehensible to the un-mechanical mind, it fetched up over its bow a small bright chain which lay along the bottom of the canal, and paying it out again over the stern, dragged itself forward, link by link, with its whole retinue of loaded skows. Until one had found out the key to the enigma, there was something solemn and uncomfortable in the progress of one of these trains, as it moved gently along the water with nothing to mark its advance but an eddy alongside dying away into the wake.'[46]

Stevenson was delighted by the sight of these canal barges with their sails high above the treetops and the windmill, sailing through green cornlands and over aqueducts: 'and to see the barges waiting their turn at a lock, affords a fine lesson of how easily the world may be taken. There should be many contented spirits on board, for such a life is both to travel and to stay at home.' And so Stevenson concluded he would rather be a bargee than occupy any position that required attendance at an office.

After a difficult picnic lunch when the cooking apparatus failed to overcome half a gale—'from that time forward the Etna voyaged like a gentleman in the locker of the *Cigarette*'—the pair paddled on through a 'fine green fat landscape or rather a mere green water lane, going on from village to village. Things had a settled look, as in places long lived in.'

At the last lock beyond Villevorde the lock mistress advised them that they were still a few leagues from Brussels and, as there were no beds to be had, they went on paddling in the rain: 'It fell in straight parallel lines; and the surface of the canal was thrown up into an infinity of little crystal fountains'. They reached Laeken where 'the rain took off' and met with a very friendly reception from members of the Royal Sport Nautique, who were impressed by the quality of their canoes—'Were they made by Searle & Son?', they enquired. The club's members were all employed in commerce during the day, but in the evening 'voyez vous nous sommes serieux'.

Even so, R.L.S. was not quite as *au fait* with the boating fraternity as his host, and after three stricken hours he appreciated the order for their bedroom candles, since efforts to change the subject of boats and boat races had proved fruitless and he had had to perform elaborate mime to explain features of British oarsmanship. 'Ah yes', they said, 'vous avez le sliding seat'. (First used by both crews in the Oxford and Cambridge boat race of 1873.) When the young man was gone they countermanded their candles and ordered brandy. The Royal Nautical sportsmen were 'as nice young fellows a man would wish to see, but a trifle too young and a thought too nautical for us'.

To avoid the 55 locks between Brussels and Charleroi and the frightening thought of being matched against the champion canoeist of Europe who was due to arrive at any moment, the pair decided to take their canoes by train across the frontier to the fortified town of Maubeuge. Here they were delayed, their canoes being stuck in the custom house, and were soon bored—in spite of lodging at the *Grand Cerf*, 'a very good inn, but there was nothing to do, nothing to see'.*

As MacGregor had found in Germany and the Baltic some 10 years earlier, the arrival of a man in a canoe aroused great interest at most places he visited. Stevenson and Simpson now found that about three in the afternoon the whole establishment of the *Grand Cerf* accompanied them to the water's edge.

However, no sooner had they started than the rain began; the wind was contrary and blew in furious gusts. The countryside was blighted with factory chimneys, ironworks and sordid workshops. The going was not easy. At Hautmont the lock was well-nigh impossible, due to the landing place being steep and high. A gang of grimy workmen cheerfully lent them a hand. The sun came forth, the wind dropped. The river, bordered with sedge and water flowers, wound among low hills; meadows filled with black and white cattle, orchards, hedges of great height woven about the trunks of hedgerow elms, fishermen there were in plenty and all was quiet.

As evening fell they reached the lock at Quartes and found rooms for the night at an alehouse in Pont sur Sambre, where they were taken for a couple of pedlars and accommodated in 'a double bedded pen in the loft of the house, furnished beside the beds with exactly three hat pegs and one table'. There was not so much as a glass of water, but on going downstairs in the morning the landlady pointed out two pails of water behind the street door. Unlike MacGregor, Stevenson and Simpson were diffident in proclaiming themselves canoeists and their modesty did perhaps account for their often less than warm reception at various inns. So it proved the next day, for when the 'good folk of the inn' saw two dainty little boats with a fluttering Union Jack on each, and all the varnish shining from the sponge, they were 'overcome with marvelling' and 'began to perceive that they had entertained angels unawares'. The landlady stood upon the bridge, probably lamenting that she had charged so little; the son ran to and fro calling out the neighbours to enjoy the sight, and the canoeists paddled away from quite a crowd of rapt observers. 'These gentlemen pedlars indeed! Now you see their quality too late.'

The weather continued showery 'with occasional drenching plumps'. They skirted the forest of Mormal, the rain in squirts, the wind in squalls. Only Simpson had a mackintosh and the showers inevitably began whenever they were portaging the canoes round a lock. Eventually the pair reached a lock some way before Landrecies, where Stevenson refused to go on and sat in a drift of rain to have a reviving pipe. Here he encountered a vivacious old man who, hearing of their journey, claimed it was the silliest enterprise he had ever heard of and suggested that young Stevenson should get into a train and go back home to his parents. Two youths then appeared who took R.L.S. to be Simpson's servant, and asked him many questions about his place and master's character. R.L.S. replied, as might have Sancho Panza, that his master was a good enough fellow but had this absurd voyage on the head. 'Oh, no, no', said one, 'you must not say that; it is not absurd; it is very courageous of him.' And so these admirable young men quickly dispelled Stevenson's bad humour. Recounting the affair to his friend, Simpson drily commented that

* A recent *Guide Michelin* lists no accommodation now.

58. *Le Grand Cerf* at Maubeuge, 1904. Stevenson and Sir Walter Simpson lodged for some days awaiting the arrival of the canoes from Brussels by train. 'It seemed to be inhabited principally by soldiers and bagmen. We had good meals, which was a great matter; but that was all.'

they must have a curious idea of how English servants behave—'for you treated me like a brute beast at the lock'.

At the garrison town of Landrecies the rain still fell and the wind continued unabated, but they found a good inn and, although the weather forced them to stay a day longer than they wished, at least it gave 'hundreds of persons' the opportunity to see the two canoes in a coal shed. They dined with a local JP, a collector of brass warming-pans, but the conversation followed more the law than boating experiences. The rain continued in a manner rarely attained outside the Scottish Highlands, but in some sort of drizzle they set off along the Sambre & Oise Canal. Here lay long lines of barges, some with gay iron railings and many looking mighty spruce and shipshape. R.L.S. was much impressed by these little canal cities with 'their flower-pots and smoking chimneys, their washings and dinners', and soon found the opportunity to look over one of these water villas whose owners kept three birds in a cage and remembered the Englishmen who the previous year (1875) had come up the canal in a steamer. This was Mr Moens in the *Ytene* (*see* Chapter IX).

59. Barges on the Sambre & Oise Canal, *c.* 1908

From Etreux the canoes were carted through a valley of hop-gardens and the village of Tupigny to Vadencourt, where they were launched from a little lawn opposite a mill into the swollen Oise. The river was in flood after the heavy rains and Stevenson described their fast trip down to Origny in excellent style:

'The water was yellow and turbulent, swung with an angry eddy among half-submerged willows, and made an angry clatter along stony shores. The course kept turning and turning in a narrow and well-timbered valley. Now, the river would approach the side, and run gliding along the chalky base of the hill, and show us a few open colza fields among the trees. Now, it would skirt the garden-walls of houses, where we might catch a glimpse through a doorway, and see a priest pacing in the chequered sunlight. Again, the foliage closed so thickly in front, that there seemed to be no issue; only a thicket of willows, overtopped by elms and poplars, under which the river ran flush and fleet, and where a kingfisher flew past like a piece of the blue sky. On these different manifestations, the sun poured its clear and catholic looks. The shadows lay as solid on the swift surface of the stream as on the stable meadows. The light sparkled golden in the dancing poplar leaves, and brought the hills into communion with our eyes. And all the while the river never stopped running or took breath; and the reeds along the whole valley stood shivering from top to toe.'[47]

After a stroll on shore and a smoke, they paddled on. 'The river was more danger-ous here; it ran swifter, the eddies were more sudden and violent. All the way down we had had our fill of difficulties. Sometimes it was a weir which could be shot, sometimes one so shallow and full of stakes that we must withdraw the boats from the water and carry them round. But the chief sort of obstacle was a consequence of the late high winds. Every two or three hundred yards a tree had fallen across the river and usually involved more than another in its fall.' And soon the *Arethusa* swung broadside on as Stevenson attempted to pass under a fallen tree, leaned over, tipped him into the stream and thus disencumbered, floated on, necessitating Simpson having a hard paddle to recover it. (Stevenson wrote four days later that 'my boat culbutted me under a fallen tree in a very rapid current; and I was a good while before I got on to the outside of that fallen tree; rather a better while than I cared about. When I got up, I lay some time on my belly, panting, and exuded fluid'.[48]) Darkness had fallen when they at length reached Origny Sainte-Benoite with R.L.S. shivering like the reeds.

There were quite a number of interested observers who came to look over the canoes which had been housed for the night in a coach-house, but not perhaps as large a number as MacGregor attracted a decade earlier. Requested to name the hour of their departure on the morrow, they felt a crowd, however friendly, was undesir-able and gave a time while mentally determined to start a few hours earlier. The pair saw a large balloon floating above the village which had come from Saint Quentin and many of the villagers joined them in running up the hill in the hope of seeing it land. At the inn the company at table treated them to sparkling wine and they had a lively discussion with three Frenchmen, two from the north and the landlady's husband.

In spite of the false scent, there were some 50 people about the bridge to witness their departure, including three young ladies who picked up their skirts and chased along the riverbank until they were out of breath; the foremost of the three leaped up on a tree stump and boldly kissed her hand to the canoeists. 'Come back again', she cried, 'and all the others echoed her.'

Even though in flood, the upper reaches of the Oise* were no more than a wind-ing rushing stream with numerous obstacles in the form of mills, sandbanks and fallen trees. After three hours' paddling the canoeists were still on the outskirts of Origny, so when they arrived at the point where the river disappeared in a syphon

---

* Moens had the previous year observed that the width of the Oise further downstream near La Fère was no more than six feet wide, its course marked with pollard willows and rushes.

beneath the Sambre & Oise canal they transferred to the water and were soon at Moy.

That night they found excellent entertainment at the *Golden Sheep*, whose public rooms were embellished by German shells from the siege of La Fère as well as by Nuremberg figures, goldfish and all manner of knick-knacks. After lingering in Moy the next morning, they made a very short day of it to La Fère, another fortified town in a plain. Here they had been advised of a good hostelry bearing the name of some woodland animal, but on arriving at this capital inn the landlady, after surveying the damp and dishevelled pair from head to foot, told them they would find beds in the suburbs. 'We are too busy for the likes of you.' Simpson commented, 'We have been taken for pedlars again. Good God. What it must be to be a pedlar in reality.'

And so they set off looking for fresh lodgings and a meal on a damp inclement night and were at last rewarded by coming upon, at the other end of town by the gate, the house of '*Bazin, aubergiste, loge à pied*'. They were warmly received and as the night wore on they sat in front of the door talking softly to the innkeeper. Stevenson was delighted at the change in their fortunes and hoped that the family knew how much he liked them and appreciated their hospitality.

From La Fère 'of wicked memory' the Oise runs through open pastoral country called the Golden Valley. Steep banks bordered the manufacturing district about

60. Bazins' inn at La Fère, 1904. 'Little did the Bazins know how much they served us.' One of their daughters kept on the café after Madame Bazin died in 1907

Cluny and then they came to Noyon which stands about a mile from the river. Celebrated for its twin-towered cathedral which overlooked the *Hotel du Nord* and Stevenson's bedroom, R.L.S. was much affected by his attendance at their service and by 'the sweet groaning thunder of the organ'. 'If ever I join the Church of Rome, I shall stipulate to be Bishop of Noyon on the Oise.'

From Noyon the rain was 'incessant, pitiless, beating', all the way to Pimprez, where they lunched in sombre mood at a little inn and determined that if the rain continued to put the boats on the train. The weather took the hint and the scenery improved. The Oise joined the Aisne and the canal joined the river and they found themselves again in company with the barges they had encountered earlier. They reached Compiègne on 8 September, and disembarked at a floating laundry where the washerwomen were still beating the clothes in spite of it being past sunset. Here they put up at a big bustling hotel where 'nobody observed our presence'. Indeed, even the unassuming Robert Louis was rather put out that so little note was taken of them—except by the washerwomen!

R.L.S. was entranced by the town hall, 'all turreted and gargoyled and slashed, and bedizened with half a score of architectural fancies'. In particular, he admired the clock above the statue of Louis XII, above which three mechanical figures with cavalier-type flapping hats, each armed with a hammer, chimed out the hours, the halves and the quarters.

By now they had floated into civilisation and missed the intimacy of canoeing on a small rural river. After landing at Creil, towards sundown they reached Precy with its plain of poplars. 'In a wide luminous curve, the Oise lay under the hillside.' They stayed at a 'terrible' inn—'not even in Scotland have I found worse fare'—but were at least rewarded with the attraction of a wandering marionette show. However, the performance of Pyramus and Thisbe in five acts proved very dismal entertainment to R.L.S., although the villagers seemed delighted.

For two more days Stevenson and his companion paddled on through pleasant river landscapes enlivened by the blue dresses of the washerwomen and the blue blouses of the fishermen. At L'Isle Adam they met dozens of pleasure boats 'outing it for the afternoon, and there was nothing', as R.L.S. pointed out, 'to distinguish the true voyager from the amateur'. By now the voyage had lost its fascination, and Stevenson grew weary of his paddling, so that a letter awaiting him at Pontoise, a few miles short of the Seine, decided them to abandon the trip. Stevenson and Simpson returned to Grez.*

Stevenson's account of his canoe trip through Belgium and France was no epic, but it has become a classic; it was his first book and was published five years before he achieved fame with *Treasure Island*. Initially it had only a very moderate sale, but after the publication of Stevenson's next book, *Travels with a Donkey in the Cevennes* (1879), the popularity of *An Inland Voyage* gradually increased. Indeed, it has been published, if not so enthusiastically read, time and time again in more editions than even MacGregor's Rob Roy exploits. (The tenth edition appeared in 1899.) To some people this may be surprising, but the fact is, of course, that the book is read more for its style than for its matter, and its style is fresh and vigorous.

---

* An Epilogue was added to later editions of *An Inland Voyage*, although it first appeared in book form in 1892 in *Across the Plains*. This recounted how, while Stevenson and Simpson were walking up the valley of the Loing in 1875, R.L.S. was arrested by the gendarmerie of Chatillon sur Loire as a suspicious vagrant, on account of his penurious dress.

61. Walter Crane's frontispiece to *An Inland Voyage*, published in 1878

It is perhaps strange that so celebrated a book as *An Inland Voyage* is not a book with which today's pleasure boater is particularly familiar. Such passages like, 'In sparsely inhabited places we make all we can of each encounter; but when it comes to a city we keep to ourselves, and never speak unless we have trodden on a man's toes', speak for themselves.

Another reason is doubtless the number of school editions published during the first half of this century, in which passages were recommended for studying and such other tests as might well turn a boy's affection for a book to disfavour, so that in later years while he may remember *Three Men in a Boat* with delight he recalls *An Inland Voyage* with something of a shiver.

Even so, the book is a delightful account of wet-weather boating. 'You may paddle all day long but it is when you come back at nightfall, and look in at the familiar room, that you find Love or Death awaiting you beside the stove; and the most beautiful adventures are not those we go to seek.'

In 1904 Mr J. A. Hammerton followed the route of *An Inland Voyage* on a bicycle. He found the *juge de paix* of Landrecies married and Monsieur Bazin dead, although his widow still kept the inn.[49] In 1928 the Headmaster of Leeds Modern School, G. F. Morton, wrote 'To attempt to follow in the canoe steps of R.L.S. in the valley of the Sambre and the Oise is today a bewilderment and a confusion.'[50] Indeed, the whole country described in the book was much affected by the Great War. Stevenson's words about Landrecies were prophetic: 'It was just the place to hear the round going by at night in the darkness, with the solid tramp of men marching, and the startling reverberations of the drum. It reminded you, that even this place was a point in the great warfaring system of Europe, and might on some future day be ringed about with cannon smoke and thunder, and make itself a name among strong towns.'[51] Some 40 years later, on 25 August 1914, the town was the scene of a sharp fight when the Guards Brigade was attacked by the German vanguard issuing from the forest of Mormal. The forest itself divided the British retreat in the autumn of 1914, and was partly the scene of the battle for the Hindenburg defences in October 1918. By the end of the war the forest had all but vanished.

The war front of 1914–17 lay between Compiègne and Noyon. Noyon itself, entered by the Germans on 1 September 1914, was, after the battle of the Aisne in October 1914 till the German offensive of the spring of 1918, the nearest occupied town to Paris, some 62 miles distant. M. Clemenceau was fond of reiterating: 'Messieurs les Allemands sont encore à Noyon.' The town was taken and retaken seven times in as many days, its villas and hotels destroyed, its cathedral bombed, the trees along its boulevards cut down. Of the cathedral, built in the late 12th century, only one damaged tower and the walls of the nave remained. Maubeuge held out against the invaders from 25 August to 7 September 1914. The inn at Pont sur Sambre was blown to bits; so, too, the chateau and the *Golden Sheep* of Moy. 'La Fère of cursed memory' was abandoned to the Germans in 1914 and formed part of their front line after the retreat on the Somme in March 1917. It was mostly destroyed. Compiègne was occupied by the Germans for a few days in September 1914; and finally, 4½ miles east of it, the armistice was signed.

It was not the outlandish weather that limited Stevenson's boating accounts to this one voyage, but penury and ill health. So enamoured of life on the water were R.L.S. and Simpson, of progressing leisurely from place to place, that they projected for themselves an old age on the canals of Europe. 'It was to be the most leisurely of progresses, now on a swift river at the tail of a steamboat, now waiting horses for days together on some inconsiderable junction. We should be seen pottering on deck in all the dignity of years, our white beards falling into our laps. We were ever to be busied among paintpots; so that there should be no white fresher, and no green more emerald than ours, in all the navy of the canals. There should be books in the cabin, and tobacco jars, and some old Burgundy as red as a November sunset and as odorous as a violet in April.' This idea, conceived by the sight of barges on the Seine & Oise canal, germinated into some degree of fulfilment. In 1877 Stevenson abandoned his plan for another canoe voyage from the Loing to the Mediterranean via the Rhône, and with Walter Simpson and two companions bought a barge which they christened the *Eleven Thousand Virgins of Cologne*.* Moored on the Loing under the walls of the ancient town of Moret, Monsieur Maltras, the 'accomplished' local carpenter, was engaged to convert her into a pleasure boat.

The project came to an untimely end when funds ran out. The barge was left to rot in the stream until finally she was 'auctioned by the 'indignant' carpenter, together with the two canoes, *Arethusa* and *Cigarette*.'† 'Now', wrote Stevenson, 'these historic vessels fly the tricolour and are known by new and alien names.'[53]

Stevenson first met Mrs Fanny Osbourne at Grez on his return from the inland voyage. In May 1880 they were married in San Francisco and returned to Europe. However, Stevenson had several severe bouts of illness and finally suffered a complete breakdown in health. He and his wife left their home at Bournemouth in 1887 for America and the South Seas. He died seven years later in Western Samoa. He was 44.

* Suggested by Venetian painter Vittore Carpaccio (1455–1522) whose set of frescoes illustrated the life and martyrdom of St Ursula and the Eleven Thousand Christian Maidens.

† In the summer of 1878 the impecunious Stevenson had set off into the Cevennes with a donkey with the aim of finding material for another book, and his illness in America the following year put paid to his barge dream. Philip Hamerton wrote to Stevenson in August 1880 suggesting that he might like to join him on a voyage on the Saone but R.L.S. sadly replied that chronic illness did not permit him to accept.

Chapter XII

HAMERTON AND JOSEPH PENNELL ON THE SAONE (1886)

Plans for a voyage on the Rhône fail—Hamerton builds a catamaran for boating on the Saone —R. L. Stevenson invited to join a cruise—Seeley's agree to a book on the Saone—hire of the Boussemroum—the originality of the craft—converted into a houseboat—towed by steamer from Chalon to Corre—Joseph Pennell joins the boat at Gray—his opinion of Hamerton— tunnels on the Upper Saone—spy fever—arrested by the gendarmerie—Pennell departs at Chalon—Hamerton resumes voyage downstream in his catamaran—reaches the Ile Barbe above Lyons—returns to Macon—publication of The Saone; A Summer Voyage *(1887)—the book's limited success—Hamerton's death (1894).*

HAMERTON'S second boating book was quite a different affair from his first (*see* Chapter V). In the intervening 20 or so years since his voyage on the 'Unknown River' he had continued to live in Burgundy and had become increasingly well-known as a writer and art critic.

His book *Round my House* (1876) told the story of his life in France and his love of boating which he shared with his two sons, for whom he designed and had built all manner of craft. As his wife described in her biography, 'He and his brother-in-law Charles went exploring these "unknown" streams and generally came home dripping wet, having abandoned their canoes in the entanglement of roots and weeds after a sudden upset, and having to go and fetch them back with a cart.' Typically, his diary for October 1875 records two trips on the Arroux to Laisy and Etang. 'We had no accidents except on a little sunken rock after Chaseux when M. de Fontenay's boat was upset.'

For many years Hamerton hankered to do a book on the Rhône whose scenery he much admired, but Richmond Seeley his publisher could not be persuaded, and thought such a trip should begin at the Rhône glacier and end at the Mediterranean which was rather further than the author intended. Finally, a compromise was reached and Seeley conceded that a well-illustrated book about the Saone might be successful. Its execution, however, suffered numerous frustrations.

One problem was the type of boat to be used for the voyage. In 1879 Hamerton had had designed and built a wooden catamaran which could sleep two or three passengers on deck in tents. However, the first trial in August 1880 ended in disaster, when she sank at anchor at Chalon whilst her captain was dining ashore. The *Morvandelle* was raised, given an iron hull and a voyage was planned on the Saone for the following summer. Hamerton proposed that Robert Louis Stevenson should accompany him and suggested that they might collaborate on a book.* R.L.S. replied from Pitlochry (Perthshire) that chronic illness prevented him from accepting such an envious cruise but that he was glad to hear that the catamaran was on her

---

* R.L.S., who was a contributor to *The Portfolio*, had visited the Hamertons unexpectedly one day in 1878; 'just happened to call without previous notice' and spent the afternoon with them. 'What a bright winning youth he was', wrote Eugenie Hamerton; 'what a delightful talker ... he seemed like a friend immediately'. Mrs Hamerton also recalled that she had been charmed by reading *An Inland Voyage*, and how she had feared that 'such a delicate and refined talent' would not bring popularity to the author.

legs again and he would 'continue to hope for a better time, canoes that will sail better to the wind and a river grander than the Saone'.[54]

In September, Hamerton again took his sons, Stephen and Richard, sailing on the Saone from Chalon to Tournus and then with Richard down to Macon. 'A beautiful voyage it was. The loveliest weather, favourable wind, strong, delightful play of light and colour on the water. I had not enjoyed such boating since I left Loch Awe.'

In August 1882 Robert Browning, to whom Hamerton had written while cruising, replied, 'my little word of thanks in reply would never get well under weigh from the banks of our sluggish canal' [the Regent's Canal], so he had waited until reaching Isère. In August 1883 Hamerton went with his elder son Stephen and nephew Maurice Pelletier for a 10-day cruise on the Saone in his new catamaran *L'Arar*, which proved a success. The following April Hamerton, his wife and daughter, sailed by steamer from Chalon to Macon and Lyons. The author noted in his diary that 'we passed through some lovely scenery, but I came to the conclusion never to boat with the *Arar* below Courzon'.

Indeed, this trip finally convinced Hamerton that his Rhône project was impracticable and he decided to go ahead with the book on the Saone. Seeley's agreed that Hamerton should write the text and that Joseph Pennell, the young American artist, should be asked to do the illustrations since the author would not have time enough to do it adequately himself. In addition, Hamerton invited his good friend Captain Kornprobst, a retired French Army officer from Alsace with a pronounced German accent, who had fought in the Crimea and had been wounded in the Franco-Prussian War, to act as purser.

Hamerton's Saone adventure was planned not only to allow him to write an account of a voyage which he believed 'no Englishman or American ever before made', but to get on with his other work. And, since there was no accommodation for tourists on the river between Corré and Chalon, Hamerton (now in his fifties) decided that the most satisfactory way of combining work and pleasure would be to hire a steamer. In this he failed, and it seemed that he might have to use his catamaran, when the hire of a berrichon* was suggested. By the end of May 1886 such a craft had been hired together with its owner and his donkey. This uncommon craft was some 80 feet long, had a flat bottom and an interior beam of 7 ft. 2½ ins. The hull was divided into compartments which provided ample space for three tents although the length of the interior was interrupted by the donkey house, which stretched from bulwark to bulwark, and by the adjoining hay store.

The contrivances erected on board the *Boussemroum* for the accommodation of the author, artist and purser were quite ingenious. From being a long canal boat, it was converted into a houseboat by the erection of a camp inside it. Each tent—relics from the author's camp life in Scotland—was provided with an iron bedstead and chair, paper ewer and basin, chest, table and Japanese matting on the oak floor. A quarter deck with an awning and camp stools provided an area for viewing and relaxation. The largest tent on the deck formed the saloon which served as the dining room and library† and boasted the sole armchair. Here, when the weather was bad, Hamerton read or worked comfortably writing chapters for *Imagination in Landscape Painting* and *French & English*, as well as the series of letters to Seeley

---

* These boats were built for use on the canals of Berri where the locks used to be narrow but were widened in the mid-19th century.

† A bookcase containing some 50 volumes including Stevenson's *An Inland Voyage*.[55]

62. Zoulou emerging from the donkey-house on board the *Boussemroum*

in which form his book on the Saone was to appear. Meantime, Kornprobst and Pennell kept to their own tents.

The crew, whose berths were in the poop cabin, consisted of the barge-owner Vernet, known as the Patron, who proved to be a competent cook, Horace the pilot, who did the steering, and a fatherless boy Franki, who joined the boat at Corré to look after the donkey. Franki slept in a tiny tent on a pile of straw.

The voyage began on the first of June with the berrichon being loaded with the camp paraphernalia and baggage at the canal basin at Chalon sur Saone. The *Boussemroum* was then brought down the canal to the river, with only a 3-inch clearance beneath some of the bridges. From here they were towed to Corré by screw steamer in company with two heavily-laden and two empty barges as well as another berrichon carrying coal.

The voyage upstream was uneventful. Joseph Pennell joined the boat at Gray. Hamerton had painstakingly written to him advising exactly what clothes to bring, about drawing paper, rugs, the geography of the river, and timetables, and had remarked 'Seeley tells me you do not swim. Would it not be a nice precaution to have an inflatable waistcoat and inflatable life belt? My boat is perfectly safe, but you may fall into the water by accident and I cannot promise to fish you out, and if I didn't, Mrs Pennell would never forgive me.' And he even wrote to her to say that he would look after her 26-year-old husband.

Pennell had not expected to sleep under canvas (he had been allocated the smallest of the three tents!) but, wrote Hamerton, he 'accepted his fate with a cheerfulness that did him credit'. This friendly comment by Hamerton is remarkable in that he made little mention of his feelings for the artist during the remainder of the voyage!* Yet Hamerton was full of praise for his enthusiasm and love of sketching and had formed a genuine liking for Pennell, writing to Gilder of the Century to explain why that firm should loan him their employee and stating that he didn't know any artist that he would like so much and that he would not enter into an engagement with anyone else. Hamerton did, however, later remark that they shared a liking for gipsies and that Pennell was 'young and energetic, and an American, and has not yet accepted the consolatory doctrine of middle age that the enforced halts of life are nature's own havens of tranquility'.

In 1925 Joseph Pennell devoted a chapter of his autobiography *The Adventures of an Illustrator* to his voyage on the Saone. It is an interesting account and confirms what many readers of *The Saone* might have guessed; that the adventures Hamerton recorded were from his point of view but 'scarce from' Pennell's. Hamerton had his cabin and his books and his lamp, but Pennell had a tent, and he was not used to tents, particularly ones which made a sort of basin which caught the rain and which overflowed when the occupier turned in his sleep! Furthermore, although Hamerton was 'delightful and kind, there was something about him—he did not just come off. Everything with him was like the *Boussemroum*, arranged according to his theory. He loved camping, and sailing, and art too. But there was through it all a something, a want of humour, of fun, a deadly seriousness that was his great enemy and barrier and defect.' Pennell and Kornprobst would spend night after night in Hamerton's cabin in serious talk, and 'sometimes there was even a petit verre de kirsch which we bought from the lock-keepers who made it. But as we left his cabin, the Captain would whisper as we made our way back to our windy tents—'allons au café', and after a brandy would say 'Il est charmant, mais, mon cher, quel type!' And so, although Hamerton lived, was married and died in France, he did not really share the Frenchman's exuberant love of wine and good food, and he evidently took himself a little too seriously.

The convoy of barges travelled only by day and Corré was not reached until the eighth of June. The main cause of delay was the locks, since at each the train of boats had to be disconnected. The dark brown donkey, Zoulou, hardly moved from his stable, cruising as did Stevenson's Etna cooker, 'like a gentleman'.

Corré was then a picturesque village of some six hundred inhabitants which formed, as it still does, the head of the navigation, since here the river was joined by the Saone & Meuse canal and thus linked to the canal systems of Belgium and Holland. Hamerton and Pennell spent three days sketching a variety of views while the *Boussemroum* lay moored close to a fine park.

The 150-mile voyage down the Upper Saone to Chalon was begun on 11 June. This stretch of the navigation included 16 lock cuts, none more than two miles long but which included—rare features for a river navigation—two tunnels at Ovanches and Savoyeux.

The voyage is described in some detail. The grand sweeping curves of the Saone, passing below steep richly-wooded hills, made it a painter's river with well-coloured foregrounds and beautiful blue distances. But there was a multitude of other interesting features to sketch. The public fountains and houses at Ormoy, the ruined

---

* Hamerton was 25 years his senior. The only other recorded dialogue not pertaining to sketching was Pennell's comment on Franki's wages. 'This', said Mr Pennell, 'is clearly a case of slave-dealing, the difference being that you would never in the Southern States have got such a boy for so little money.' Hamerton ventured to disagree. However, besides looking after the donkey, Franki peeled potatoes, shelled peas and cleaned shoes excellently.

castle at Cendrecourt, a modernised one at Chemilly, barns, country houses, picturesque streets, multi-arched bridges, a ferry near Jussey, all made interesting subjects
for Pennell's pen.

After passing the picturesque village of Conflandey, they observed the towpath
cut into the towering sides of a steep rocky shore, but they had problems approaching the little town of Port-sur-Saone as the strong gusty wind drove their lightly-
laden boat ashore time and again. At Scey they moored in the canal basin whose
surface was adorned with yellow waterlilies and which lay opposite a fine avenue
of towering poplars. Hamerton went into town to buy the donkey boy a present of
socks and shoes since his sockless feet were blistered by wearing boots.

63. The *Boussemroum* in the basin at Scey on the Saone, 1886

There was quite a lot of barge traffic on the river. Although the *Boussemroum*
was an odd-looking affair with its encampment draped across the deck and bulwarks,
it did not, however, excite undue curiosity from the river people accustomed to all
types of huts and 'tendues' on their craft. The largest type of boat on the Saone was
the péniche, whose tonnage varied from 150 to 320 tons. Hamerton noted that there
was often a commodious stable for the horses and a huge lug sail for when the horses
were on board; also that the cabins had persienne shutters on the windows and
curtains of white lace or embroidered muslin.

Describing the novel experience of passing through the tunnel near Ovanches, Hamerton wrote 'An impressive contrast awaited us when we had to turn aside from this golden sunshine, these cheerful pictures of cattle grazing in happy pastures under beautiful groups of trees, or merry peasants passing in the ferry-boat—and we came to the gloomy portals of a tunnel. We came upon it suddenly as we turned aside from the pleasant river and saw close before us the grim entrance, with its severe monumental architecture, its sad-looking firs and pines standing on each side, silent on the green sward, all dark in the shadow of the hill. There was nothing to help us through the dark vault but the very slowest of all imaginable streams, produced artificially by a partial opening of the water-gates beyond. By an almost imperceptible motion this stream took us into the darkness, and then, for our encouragement, it tranquilly sent us back again. After what seemed an interminable delay, the stream slowly drew us a second time under the vault, and then, as if to make us forget our lugubrious surroundings, the Patron cheerfully announced dinner. The saloon was lighted, the blind drawn, and we tried to make-believe that we were dining exactly as usual. It is impossible, however, to forget one's surroundings, and for my part I find tunnels depressing to the imagination. After this tunnel the canal sweeps round a long majestic curve between fine stone quays, and above these is a steep slope on each side of well-kept grass, planted with fir-trees. Emerging from this cutting, which is more like English 'grounds' than anything else, the canal goes in a straight line to the lock, and the country is open on both sides. This canal is a short cut across a large peninsula, where the Saone makes a curve of six miles. In this peninsula are two or three villages and one of them is Ovanches.'

There were numerous occasions when Hamerton was enraptured by the beauty of the scene, none more so than when after leaving Scey he wrote 'The time was late afternoon, with golden sunshine, the scenery a reach or two of calm river, reflecting shores all beautiful with rock and tree and freshest verdure.'

There were also less harmonious occasions when the pilot told the owner how incompetent he was to manage a boat, a truth which Hamerton felt might be repeated too frequently. Indeed, they often quarrelled and as the pilot was much the bigger man, Pennell was apprehensive of the fate of the smaller who couldn't swim, should he be thrown into the water. However, both men were indispensable and Hamerton as captain took each of the men aside and by threatening to terminate the expedition, peace would be re-established for a time.

The narrative is full of interesting little points. Hamerton raptured about the village and castle of Ray, spoke sternly to a lock-keeper whose nine-year-old son was playing by the lock and had not yet learnt to swim, walked over the tunnel at Savoyeux, made the acquaintance of the ferryman at Quitteur, feared an accident when the *Boussemroum* narrowly missed the wire rope of the ferry at Prantigny, met with uncommon incivility from the bargemen of a péniche because the boat was in their way, lunched dismally inside the deep lock at Rigny, admired the approach to Gray and its Spanish character, enjoyed the scenery to Mantoche, beyond which place Zoulou actually overtook a boat drawn by horses, admired the riverside lawns and gardens of Pontailler where the voyage might have terminated if events had not taken a favourable turn.

Now relations between France and Prussia continued to be strained during the 1880s and it was perhaps a little unfortunate that at the time of Hamerton's voyage France was in another grip of spy fever. A regulation had only recently been passed empowering the police to arrest any person found sketching military objects and such works as roads, canals and bridges. At Corré a pair of gendarmes had observed Kornprobst watching Hamerton sketching and 10 days later a tunnel guard near Savoyeux had ominously approached them to say that he had received a telegram enquiring about their nationality. Then quite suddenly they were arrested.

The day after reaching Pontailler, the *Boussemroum* was boarded by four gend-armes, one of whom was remarkably aggressive. They were interrogated; their drawings were seized and taken away to Dijon for examination. Meanwhile, two armed guards remained behind to keep the party under surveillance.

Only prompt action by Mrs Hamerton on hearing the news, and a telegram from the Minister of War obtained their release and the return of the drawings the following day. However, before the berrichon was allowed to continue on its way, artist and author were told by the local authorities not to sketch military works, particularly the fortifications of Auxonne which lay downstream.

Hamerton observed that they were watched whenever they disembarked and lugubriously concluded that 'an artist must in all cases make up his mind to be interrogated and perhaps occasionally arrested and detained for a short time'. Moreover, he finally and rather reluctantly decided that while voyaging in the *Boussemroum* was pleasant enough, a houseboat was the dullest variety of nagi-gation and it was far from ideal due to the stoppages caused by the wind buffeting the superstructure which without its normal cargo of coal stood six feet out of the water and forced it into the river bank. It was all one poor donkey could do to avoid being pulled into the river and constant pushes with a pole were required to keep the keel from grounding on the bank. On one occasion near Corré the boat struck the bank every minute or so with a shock which made writing or drawing impossible.

64. Donkey towage proved inadequate for so large a barge only lightly laden

Hamerton, therefore, had the berrichon towed by tug from Pontailler past Aux-onne to St Jean de Lorne (whose 23 miles were covered in nine hours), and again from there to Verdun, a further 30 miles. Poor Zoulou had done his bit but he could not pull such a huge craft when there was a cross-wind. At Verdun, Korn-probst had to take his leave; they also had a further visit from the authorities regard-ing their papers and their sketching. The final 16 miles to Chalon was covered slowly and painfully as the wind continued to push the boat into the bank. And so Hamerton decided to abandon the *Boussemroum* at Chalon, pay off the crew and proposed that they should make the second part of their trip on his catamaran. However, Pennell was not too keen on the idea—he regarded the craft as 'rather like a life-raft with a sail on it'—and decided to complete the voyage downstream by public steamer. This attempt was thwarted by his failure to obtain official permission to sketch at Lyons. Rather than abandon the book, Pennell agreed to make drawings from the author's sketches although when the book came to be published 19 pen drawings were Hamerton originals. 'Pennell thought it better', wrote Hamerton to his publisher, 'that I should draw my boat itself as I understand it and he might make mistakes. I agree with him on this point.'[56]

The cruise of the lower Saone began some eight weeks later on 29 June. Hamerton used his steel-hulled catamaran, the *Arar*, 24 feet long, with a beam of 7 ft. 3 ins. and only drawing 15 inches of water, with twin 18-foot masts short enough to pass beneath the bridges. It was not an ideal craft, but when the crew of the steamer which had towed them to Corré suggested that a motor boat would be best, Hamer-ton disagreed. Besides the expense, 'there would be none of the pleasures of boating. Steadier travelling power, paid for in dirt and vibration'.

Hamerton took with him his elder son Stephen (his younger son Richard com-mitted suicide in 1888), now 27, and 18-year-old nephew, Maurice Pelletier. It was a pleasant and successful voyage but without great incident. Because the river was at its lowest and the navigation was closed for repairs, there was little traffic and as the weather was intensely hot, they sailed, rowed or towed mainly at dawn or dusk; but on one occasion the young men had to use the 85-yard tow rope from the bank throughout the day. Picnicking at La Colonne, Hamerton praised the sparkling local white wine. At Tournus they saw the 20-foot shaft of the Roman column which had been dredged from the river at La Colonne, to which place Hamerton urged that it should be restored. The weather remained fair, a clear blue sky and not a breath of wind. Leaving Tournus an hour before sunset, they rowed to Villars, a picturesque little village perched on a bluff with a 12th-century Roman-esque church. After passing the mouth of the Seille (the only navigable tributary which rises in the Jura) and Farges, they beached the boat for the night and slung two hammocks in a tent erected between the masts, while Maurice made do in a tiny tent on the poop.

The party did indeed sleep in all manner of places; a fisherman's cottage, a little rustic inn, a large hotel; and sometimes on board the *Arar*, but not often, as they only had rugs and hammocks and did not undress on board.

Pleasant evenings were spent at riverside cafés where Hamerton was well-known, and sometimes on board boat. They also lunched well at little inns like that above

65. Hamerton and his elder son Stephen in their catamaran *L'Arar* on the Saone

66. *L'Arar* moored for the night with tents erected on the deck and hammocks
slung beneath them

the suspension bridge at Fleurville, but there such delight was later tarnished on their return aboard boat by a tiresome adverse wind and short choppy waves through which they had to row the last nine miles to the island of St John. At Macon they stayed at the *Sauvage*, and Hamerton recalled that he had slept in the bed there which Napoleon had used on his return from Elba.

For four and more miles from Macon they traversed a vast green plain dotted with browsing cattle. Between the suspension bridges of St Romain and Thoissey they disturbed the solitude of a group of girls bathing, who hid themselves in the water. At Port de Belleville, where they got bedrooms in a lofty ill-kept house, Maurice left them on 11 September to prepare for an exam, 'greatly to our regret' since he had a lively and merry disposition and showed exemplary patience in bearing the delays and annoyances occasioned by dead calm, terrible heat and time spent in sketching.

Hamerton's mode of travelling must have been something of a strain for the younger men. Every member of the expedition had his appointed duties, he wrote, and he expected them to be performed with the strictest regularity. His wife recalled that he was a man who liked to 'marcher militairement'. They rose at five, breakfasted at seven, lunched at one, dined at seven and retired at ten. 'Everything has its place [in the boat] according to two systems, one called "night order" the other "day order" and each of us knows the place of each detail under the other two. There is consequently no confusion and I [Hamerton] am spared the trouble of giving directions.'[57] His style of living was founded on the principle of decency without luxury. *Vin ordinaire* was the rule and good Burgundy was reserved for 'state occasions'. Hamerton had no desire to have women or children on board; children because they would be in the way and made a noise and 'I should like to know the woman personally before entrusting my peace to her for many weeks. She might be a talker, or even a scold, she might be dirty and slovenly in her habits, all of which would spoil the pleasure of my trip completely.'[58]

Hamerton sketched Montmerle, cheered by the music from a fair, and found the scenery downstream 'very rich in wood and meadow'. Sailing with a faint breeze and enjoying the solitude of a moonlit night, they supped on bread and cheese and moored by the bridge at Beauregard. Their voyage to Trevoux was 'an enchantment. The scenery is lovely, the weather was perfectly beautiful and we had just enough wind to speed the *Arar* as fast as we care to travel.' Beyond Trevoux, Hamerton considered the great locks on the Lower Saone 'magnificent' and visited the yacht basin at Port de Neuville. By now their voyage was nearly ended. After the lock at Courzon, the Saone was transformed into a narrow curving river shaded by thickly-wooded hills. The *Arar* reached Saint Rambert and the Ile Barbe just above Lyons and its junction with the Rhône on 19 September but our ageing adventurer 'had no intention of taking her through the city to the Rhône since sailing was out of the question in a crowded water thoroughfare'.

It now only remained for Hamerton and his son to return to Macon (a voyage made easier with the help of a steam tug), where they berthed the *Arar* on 23 September. He considered the voyage a great success, the only disappointment being the persistent lack of wind.

The book appeared towards the end of 1887, bound in blue cloth with all edges gilt and with gilt-decorated illustrations on the front cover. The reviews were, according to Mrs Hamerton, 'hearty'.[59] The *Spectator* described the story as 'delightful throughout' and *The Times* praised it in similar terms. *The Saone; A Summer Voyage* did not, however, sell well and was never popular. The booksellers gave the reason that the illustrations were not etched and that the price of one guinea (£1.05) was in any case steepish. To Eugenie Hamerton its failure was 'unaccountable' and a great disappointment to both her and her husband.

It is not, however, an exceptionally interesting book, being neither particularly adventurous, humorous, nor useful as a guide. Yet it is well written in parts, profusely illustrated with some excellent drawings by Pennell, and interesting to the present-day reader in its descriptions of contemporary canal and river life. It suffers a little from repetitive passages which could have been avoided by better editing. The narrative is also uneven and interspersed with recollections of incidents on earlier voyages, particularly of that made in 1885. Nevertheless, the very nature of the voyage amply justifies its inclusion in this volume.

Hamerton's interest in boats continued to be reflected in his diary and in the articles he contributed to *Le Yacht*. His boating expeditions on the Saone continued until the family moved to Boulogne sur Seine in 1891 where he died in November 1894 aged 60. The Paris correspondent of *The Times* wrote that, although Hamerton had long-ceased to be a familiar figure on the Boulevards, 'intercourse with him was delightful. His grave humour, his wide knowledge of the literature and achievements of art, his large appreciativeness, his lack of insularity, due as much to his artist's temperament as to the fact of his having lived much abroad and travelled widely, made him a memorable companion;... It is a genial and lovable man who has gone from us, whose books have been the guide of many men of taste.'[60]

Chapter XIII

JEROME K JEROME AND *THREE MEN IN A BOAT* (1888)

Common features of boating narratives—publication of Three Men in a Boat *(1889)—authenticity of George, Harris, and Montmorency—Jerome's early life—love of boating—familiarity with the Thames—the voyage to Oxford—Moulsey lock—the river in sunlight—and in rain—cooking scrambled eggs—incongruous episodes—originality and humour of* Three Men in a Boat—*its world-wide success.*

ALL, or nearly all, boating narratives have common features. In each the crew remain anonymous even if the pseudonyms are thinly disguised; there is the plan to have a holiday afloat, the description of the type of boat, the stores carried, the food and drink consumed, the weather, the assessment of accommodation and the reception given to the adventurer as he arrives at each new place. Topographical details of the route are often interspersed with historical reminiscences, church architecture and comment on the manners and morals of the 'foreigners'.

The problem with most accounts is the lack of variety in misfortune. Troublesome gendarmes and customs officials, uncomfortable inns, surly service, poor food, wretched weather and the occasional mishap formed the sum total of most boating experiences. It was left to Jerome K Jerome (1859–1927) to produce, more by accident than design, 'the most amusing account of a pleasure cruise'.

Jerome K Jerome's *Three Men in a Boat* (to say nothing of the Dog), published by Arrowsmith in 1889, is probably the best known book on boating ever written. It is a humorous semi-autobiographical account of Jerome's excursion from Kingston to Oxford with two companions, George Wingrove and Carl Hentschel, in the early spring of 1888. Wingrove was a bank clerk who shared lodgings with Jerome in Tavistock Place, close to the British Museum, and Hentschel was a Pole whose father had introduced photo-etching into England, a process which enabled newspapers to print photographs. In the book 'J' was Jerome himself, 'George' was Wingrove, and 'Harris' was Hentschel.

'Montmorency I evolved out of my inner consciousness. Dog friends that I came to know later have told me he was true to life', wrote J.K.J. in his autobiography, although in the preface to the first edition he had indicated that the dog was also very real. Of course, it is absurd to study the facts too closely. All boating accounts, like fishermen's tales, improve with the telling and it is only the fame and locale of J.K.J.'s account which have prompted serious efforts to separate fact from fiction. There are, therefore, those who class the book as fiction but as J.K.J. stated in his preface, 'Its pages form the record of events that really happened. All that has been done is to colour them;' and later, Jerome was to write that boating up and down the Thames had been his favourite sport ever since he could afford it. 'I just put down the things that happened.'[61]

The publication of *Three Men in a Boat* brought fame to J.K.J. at the age of 30, but he had had a hard childhood. His father, a Nonconformist lay preacher, had lost most of his money in a mining venture in Staffordshire and died eight years after starting a wholesale ironmongery business in Limehouse when Jerome was still at grammar school. At 14 he became a clerk with the London & North Western Railway at Euston station, and for the next 16 years supported himself in a variety of jobs which included being a schoolmaster, journalist and both a part-time and repertory actor. His first book, *On the Stage—and Off*, was published in 1885 and brought him £5, and his successful play, *The Passing of the Third Floor Back*, also reflected what he had learnt as an actor.

Jerome was like his contemporary, Kenneth Grahame—a boat lover. His earliest recollections were of unsuccessfully attempting to row a home-made boat on the lake in Regent's Park, and as a boy he did a good deal of rafting on the water-filled quarries in suburban brickfields. Later he joined a boating club on the Lea Navigation where the threat of being thrown into the river by a barge's towline was not infrequent.

In 1888, two years after *The Idle Thoughts of an Idle Fellow* was published, Jerome married and moved to a tiny flat in Chelsea Gardens, 'up ninety-seven stairs'. Soon after the honeymoon, he and his two friends, Hentschel and Wingrove, decided upon another Thames holiday. Jerome took his notebook as F. W. Robinson, the editor of a magazine called *Home Chimes*, had indicated his willingness to publish a series of articles on the Thames. J.K.J. had it in mind to write 'The Story of the Thames' as more of a travel feature than a humorous account of boating. He knew the river well, its deep pools and hidden ways, its quiet backwaters, its sleepy towns and ancient villages. There was, however, to be 'humorous relief' from the scenery and history.

The fortnight's voyage from Kingston up to Oxford and back to Pangbourne (where persistent rain finally caused the trip to be abandoned) portrayed incidents which took place not only then, but on previous outings. Although amusing occurrences are embroidered by the raconteur, Robinson was not keen on the historical bits and the more prosaic passages were cut.

The first five chapters are concerned with plans and preparations. Then, after travelling from Waterloo by the London & South-Western Railway to Kingston-on-Thames, the crew find their boat waiting for them below the bridge. Harris, attired in a red and orange blazer, takes the sculls, J.K.J. at the tiller and the fox terrier Montmorency in the prow. George, still working in the City, is to join them that night at Shepperton.

And so it is not until Chapter VI that the voyage begins, passing 'the quaint back streets of Kingston, where they came down to the water's edge, looked quite picturesque in the flashing sunlight, the glinting river with its drifting barges, the wooded towpath, the trim-kept villas on the other side'.

The popularity of pleasure boating in the 1880s is nowhere better described than J.K.J.'s picture of Moulsey lock. From where he stood no water could be seen but only 'a brilliant triangle of bright blazers, and gay caps, and saucy hats, and many-coloured parasols, and silken rugs, and cloaks, and streaming ribbons

67. Jerome K. Jerome at the time *Three Men in a Boat* was published (1889)

and dainty whites. When looking down into the lock from the quay you might fancy it was a huge box into which flowers of every hue and shade had been thrown pell-mell, and lay piled up in a rainbow heap, that covered every corner.'

On a fine Sunday, Moulsey lock presented this appearance nearly all day long, while up the stream lay long lines of still more boats waiting their turn. Most of the inhabitants of Hampton and Moulsey dressed themselves up in boating costume to come and mooch round the lock with their dogs, to flirt and smoke and watch the boats. J.K.J. felt that 'altogether what with the caps and jackets of the men, the pretty coloured dresses of the women, the excited dogs, the moving boats, the white sails, the pleasant landscape, and the sparkling water, it is one of the gayest sights I know of near this dull old London town.'62

Girls, also, continued J.K.J., 'don't look half bad in a boat, if prettily dressed'. But a boating costume had to be practical, and J.K.J. tells the story of how it was his misfortune to go for a water picnic with two ladies who were beautifully got up in lace and silks like Watteau's young ladies smiling for Cythera.

The weather has always been, and doubtless always will be, a dominating influence on the record of boating expeditions. 'The river—with the sunlight flashing from its dancing wavelets, gilding gold the grey-green beech-trunks, glinting through the dark, cool wood paths, chasing shadows o'er the shallows, flinging diamonds from the mill-wheels, throwing kisses to the lilies, wantoning with the weirs' white water, silvering moss-grown walls and bridges, brightening every tiny townlet, making sweet each lane and meadow, lying tangled in the rushes, peeping, laughing, from each inlet, gleaming gay on many a far sail, making soft the air with glory—is a golden fairy stream.

'But the river—chill and weary, with the ceaseless raindrops falling on its brown and sluggish waters, with the sound as of a woman, weeping low in some dark chamber; while the woods, all dark and silent, shrouded in their mists of vapour, stand like ghosts upon the margin; silent ghosts with eyes reproachful, like the ghosts of evil actions, like the ghosts of friends neglected—is a spirit-haunted water through the land of vain regrets.'

The protagonists of *Three Men in a Boat* were no exception. 'The second day was exactly like the first. The rain continued to pour down and we sat, wrapped up in our mackintoshes, underneath the canvas, and drifted slowly down.' Food comes a close second preoccupation. Picnics do become boring. 'For about ten days we seemed to have been living, more or less, on nothing but cold meat, cake and bread and jam.'

It is the things which mankind has created for its convenience and pleasure which continually annoy and irritate their users; alarm clocks cease to ring, paraffin stoves refuse to light, tins of food won't open, useful gadgets hide from their would-be users or when found will not function as they should, the influence of the weather on people's attitudes. The idiosyncracies of human behaviour, well mirrored by the story of George's shirt* and Harris's attempt to cook scrambled eggs for breakfast, remind us of Stevenson's efforts with the Etna. 'He said he would cook them. It seemed from his account that he was very good at doing scrambled eggs. He often did them at picnics and when out on yachts. He was quite famous for them. People who had once tasted his scrambled eggs, so we gathered from his conversation, never cared for any other food afterwards, but pined away and died when they could not get them.

'It made our mouths water to hear him talk about the things, and we handed him out the stove and the frying-pan and all the eggs that had not smashed and gone over everything in the hamper, and begged him to begin.

'He had some trouble in breaking the eggs—or rather not so much trouble in breaking them exactly as in getting them into the frying-pan when broken, and keeping them off his trousers, and preventing them from running up his sleeve; but he fixed some half a dozen into the pan at last, and then squatted down by the side of the stove and chivied them about with a fork.

'It seemed harassing work, so far as George and I could judge. Whenever he went near the pan he burned himself, and then he would drop everything and dance round the stove, flicking his fingers about and cursing the things. Indeed, every time George and I looked round at him he was sure to be performing this feat. We thought at first that it was a necessary part of the culinary arrangements.

'We did not know what scrambled eggs were, and we fancied that it must be some Red Indian or Sandwich Islands' sort of dish that required dances and incantations for its proper cooking. Montmorency went and put his nose over it once, and the fat spluttered up and scalded him, and then *he* began dancing and cursing. Altogether it was one of the most interesting and exciting operations I have ever witnessed. George and I were both quite sorry when it was over.

* A story which apparently had been the rounds since it is also related by Mansfield in *The Water Lily on the Danube* (1853).

'The result was not altogether the success that Harris had anticipated. There seemed so little to show for the business. Six eggs had gone into the frying-pan, and all that came out was a teaspoonful of burnt and unappetizing looking mess.'[63]

There are, however, one or two passages which seem out of place in a humorous account, like the finding of the bloated body of a dog floating downstream;[64] or which jolt the reader into remembering the moral attitudes of the time, like the mention of the corpse of a young woman who had drowned in the river at Goring. J.K.J.'s reflections on the girl who had loved and sinned 'as some of us do now and then' indicate something of the struggle of Victorian gentlemen to be charitable towards the sinner of his day. 'Her family and friends naturally shocked and in-dignant, had closed their doors against her. Left to fight the world alone, with the millstone of her shame around her neck, she had sunk ever lower and lower. For a while she had kept both herself and the child on the twelve shillings a week that twelve hours' drudgery a day procured her, paying six shillings out of it for the child, and keeping her own body and soul together on the remainder.'[65]

The illustration by Frederics of this incident captures, Ophelia-like, the false picture of idyllic death. But, even after allowing for the tastes of the period, it is strange that J.K.J. should have inserted this particular incident, which strikes a discordant note; it is curious if the event actually happened that no mention is made of such an occurrence in Jerome's autobiography or Moss's biography. Such drownings were regularly reported in the press and the editor of *Home Chimes* may himself have suggested it as a warning that could never be emphasized too often to young ladies.

Three Men in a Boat received mixed reviews. Some were cruel and pompous, others haughty and condescending, or uncomprehending and dismissive. The *Saturday Post* concluded 'That it was worth doing we do not say; indeed we have a very decided opinion that it was not'. The *Punch* critic said it was written in low and vulgar slang and unintentionally praised it by saying he did not find it as funny as *The Pickwick Papers*. However, if the reviewers found no virtue in the vulgarity of the language, the public loved it. They loved it because it was written in the very way most people spoke. The well-told anecdotes were of an everyday nature, the characters incompetent and weak, with whom most readers could easily identify. J.K.J. wrote in 1909 that 'certain writers used to suggest that it was the vulgarity of the book, its entire absence of humour, that accounted for its success with the people, but one feels by this time that such suggestion does not solve the riddle'.

Three Men in a Boat is a clever and considered work, although its flippant style makes the work appear artless. Its appeal, like most classics, is universal, for the book succeeds admirably in developing the themes of the perversity of human nature and the awkwardness of objects and events. Nevertheless, it is the Jeromian humour—the wilful conspiracy of inanimate objects against human endeavour—which accounts for the book's extraordinary popularity. It has never gone out of print. The sales of the English editions exceeded three million in 1956.[66] Stranger, however, was the book's success abroad, particularly in Germany. It has been translated into most European and some Asiatic languages. Curiously enough, the book also had an enormous circulation in Russia, where it was widely pirated, which provoked Jerome in 1902 to write a long letter to *The Times*. After admitting a certain pride that Russia had shown such interest in his work, he wrote 'Of late my gratification has been considerably marred, however, by my powerlessness to prevent the issue of unauthorized translations, which, so I am assured by my Russian friends, are at the best garbled and incorrect, and at the worst original concoctions, of the merits or demerits of which I am entirely innocent, but which nonetheless are sold labelled with my name'.

J.K.J., writing in 1909 that 'the world has been very kind to this book', found himself quite unable to justify its success. 'I have written books that have appeared to me more clever, books that have appeared to me more humorous. But it is as the author of *Three Men in a Boat (to say nothing of the Dog)* that the public persists in remembering me.'[67] Jerome could hardly recall having written it; 'I remember only feeling very young and absurdly pleased with myself for reasons that concern only myself. It was summer time, and London is so beautiful in summer. It lay beneath my window a fairy city veiled in golden mist, for I worked in a room high above the chimney pots; and at night the lights shone far beneath me, so that I looked down as into an Aladdin's cave of jewels. It was during those summer months I wrote this book; it seemed the only thing to do.'[68]

Chapter XIV

OTHERS WE SHOULD MENTION

A SURVEY of 19th-century and pre-Great War boating expeditions would not be complete without allusion to some literary figures who engaged in boating and also to some less well-known accounts of cruises. Although many were manuscript logs written for the amusement of family and friends (e.g., that by Farrant), some which described newly 'discovered' waterways were published in the Royal Canoe Club's journal, *The Canoeist*, or in *The Field* and similar journals.* Others were printed in book form for private circulation or included in autobiographies, and a few for the public at large. Altogether they form a long list of varying literary value and content.

ANDERSON (R.C.) carried out a series of canoeing and camping trips with various friends in Sweden (1907), Norway and Sweden (1908), and Sweden, Finland and Russia (1909). His canoeing experiences dated from 1898 when as a boy he built a canvas canoe while at Winchester. She was followed by the *Grasshopper* (1901) and the *Earwig* (1902), both sailing canoes. After leaving Cambridge he made a 10-day trip in 1906 with a few nights' camping in a big Canadian canoe on the Basingstoke Canal, Test, Itchen and Wey navigations, 'interesting, though by no means an overwhelming success' for reasons not narrated (see *Canoeing and Camping Adventures*, 1910).

ANONYMOUS. Many accounts were initially published anonymously, including *The Cruise of the Water Lily* and *The Log of the Undine*, but either through their popularity or literary success the authors' identities have been subsequently revealed. Two which remain anonymous, but whose logs are worthy of mention, are *Bumps's trip through the Caledonian Canal in 1860* (privately printed) and *Red Rover*, whose account of a canoe cruise from Leicester to Greenhithe in 1872 was published the following year. Bumps was probably Mr Stockman, the principal assistant of George Stephenson, whose yacht made this passage.

Three in Norway written by Two of Them (1883) described a tour using Canadian canoes. The pair was later revealed to be J.A. Lees and W. J. Clutterbuck, and the book was reprinted widely in America, Europe and in 1949 in Norwegian.

There also exists an unusual account by two young men of a trip made by skiff and bicycle along the Chester–Kendal Canal in 1889.

AUBERTIN (C. J., 1876–1932) wrote a little-known but delightful account of canal travel in the pre-Great War era, which described the various happenings to a 33-foot-long houseboat being towed either by horse or by bow-hauling from the towpath (see *A Caravan Afloat* (n.d., 1916)).

---

* In 1880 John MacGregor was writing that 'some hundreds of cruises are chronicled, several of them a thousand miles in length, and in all quarters of the world. *The Field* has published several long, clever and well illustrated articles upon canoe building and sailing in 1879'. So also did *The Graphic* and *The Illustrated London News* in the 1880s.

BARNES (Eleanor) second wife of Sir Alfred Yarrow (1842–1932), the marine engineer and ship-builder. She was a keen canoeist and recounted her experiences on southern English streams in *As the Water Flows* (1920), which was well illustrated by Helen Stratton.

BIGELOW (Poultney, 1856–1954) American author, distinguished journalist and explorer who canoed down the Danube in 1891 from Donaueschingen with F. D. Millet (q.v.) and Alfred Parsons who were canoe novices and who wrote a rather different account of their voyage. His book *Paddles and Politics down the Danube* dwelt mainly on the political problems of the Austro-Hapsburg Empire.

BLACK (William, 1841–1898) described in *The Strange Adventures of a House-boat* how in 1887 he took the horse-drawn vessel he had designed from Kingston-on-Thames to Newbury via Birmingham and Bristol. Novelist and war correspondent.

BLISS (William) explored English and Welsh rivers and canals over half a century, and described his experiences in *The Heart of England by Waterway* (1933). He figured largely in Sir John Squire's paddling reminiscences *Water Music* (1939).

BONTHRON (Peter) travelled 2000 miles by motor boat through the waterways of Britain over a span of 30 years *c.* 1890–1915. Few precise dates were given for these excursions but they are interesting for being the only contemporary accounts of voyages on navigations like the Basingstoke Canal, the Rother Navigation from Midhurst, the Royal Military Canal from Iden to Sandgate, and also for the account of one of the last through excursions of the North Wilts & Berks Canal and Thames & Severn Canals (see *My Holidays on Inland Waterways* (n.d., 1916)).

'CARROLL (Lewis)' (Rev. C. L. Dodgson, 1833–1898) while a tutor at Christ Church, Oxford, entered in his diary for 4 July 1862: 'made an expedition up the river to Godstow with the three Liddells. We had tea there and did not reach Christ Church till half past eight'. It was on this occasion that the first of Alice's adventures in Wonderland were told (see S. D. Collingwood, *The Life and Letters of Lewis Carroll* (1898), p. 93).

CHURCH (Alfred J.) illustrated his recollections of boating and fishing between Henley and Oxford in *Isis and Thamesis* (1886).

CORBETT (J.) Salford councillor and borough engineer, who was a noted rowing man in the 1860s. His *River Irwell* (1907) described many Lancashire waterways and how pleasure boating had developed.

DAVIES (G. Christopher, 1849–1922) a noted yachtsman, angler, photographer and naturalist who wrote numerous articles for *The Field*, Hunt's *Yachting Magazine* and other periodicals about the Norfolk Broads, including *Norfolk Broads and Rivers or the Waterways, Lagoons and Decoys of East Anglia* (1883). His *Handbook to the Broads* (1882) which was republished over 50 times included advice to gentlemen 'to bathe only before eight o'clock in the morning. Ladies are not expected to

68. Frontispiece to *The Swan and Her Crew*, 1876, a fictional story based on Christopher Davies' intimate knowledge of the Norfolk and Suffolk rivers. The catamaran was built to explore the Broads and drew less than a foot of water

turn out before eight but after that time they are entitled to be free from any annoyance. Young men who lounge in a nude state on boats while ladies are passing may be saluted with dust shot or the end of a quant'. His stories for children included *The Swan and Her Crew* (1876) which concerned the adventures of three young naturalists who sailed the Norfolk Broads on a home-built catamaran. His cruising abroad was limited to the rivers and canals of Holland and Northern Belgium (see *Practical Boat Sailing*, 1880; *On Dutch Waterways*, 1887; *Cruising in the Netherlands*, 1894).

DOUGHTY (Henry M.) author who described his boating on the Norfolk Broads in *Summer in Broadland* (1889) and voyaged abroad with his family in a Norfolk wherry (see *Friesland Meres and through the Netherlands* (1889) and *Our Wherry in Wendish Lands*, a voyage from Friesland through the Mecklenburg Lakes to Bohemia and Dresden, 1892).

69. The wherry *Gipsy* at Haarlem, 1888

FARRANT (A.) kept a manuscript log of his 20-day cruise with three companions (including boat-builder John Salter) in August 1873 from Oxford. They rowed by canal to Leamington, by river to Tewkesbury and then by the Hereford & Gloucester Canal to Hereford and back by the Wye, the Severn and the Kennet & Avon Canal to Oxford. The locks on the Stratford-upon-Avon Navigation were semi-derelict and involved 'heavy work' when they had to make seven portages in one day. The party slept in a tent and after dinner they sang. 'Passed the evening with harmony and the social glass'; 'had harmony, both vocal and instrumental'; 'about ten we had out the music and commenced our usual concert' are typical nightly entries. Farrant's interesting handwritten log was not published until his grandson brought it to the attention of Edwin Course, who had it published by the Oakwood Press in 1977.

GORDON (The Hon. James, 1845–1868) was the first canoeist to cross the English Channel. He was Lord Aberdeen's brother and rowed for Cambridge in 1867 (weight 12 st. 3 lbs.). The *Light Blue Magazine* described how in the spring of 1868 Searle built him a sailing canoe in which he crossed the English Channel from Dover to Boulogne at night, and after taking the train to Paris, where he visited the Great Exhibition, he went on down the French rivers to the Mediterranean at Marseilles and came back via Genoa through the Italian and Swiss lakes, the Meuse and the Rhine, transporting his canoe by train from time to time. His account was published posthumously, however, for although he survived a severe ducking in the Rhine, he was apparently much exhausted by his canoe voyage. He had partially recovered when he met with a fatal accident in February 1868 'whilst cleaning his Volunteers rifle in his rooms at Cambridge'. (see *The Voyage Alone*, 1868, p. 241, and *Fifty Years of Sport at Oxford, Cambridge and the Great Public Schools*, vol. one, 1913, p. 201.)

GRAHAME (Kenneth, 1859–1932) author who, while at his Oxford prep. school, canoed along the upper reaches of the Thames at harvest time. By 1876, however, he had been introduced to sculling by Frederick Furnivall, a prodigious scholar who for many years conducted a ferocious campaign against the Amateur Rowing Association for excluding artisans from the amateur class in sculling. Furnivall was a compulsive but harmless exhibitionist, a close friend of Grahame for many years, and doubtless some of his exuberance is to be found in the character of Mr Toad.

In his story *The Rural Pan*, Grahame expressed the urge to find new sights 'pushing an explorer's prow up the remote untravelled Thame till Dorchester's stately roof broods over the quiet fields'. He knew the Thames, its tributaries and backwaters, and it was the river between Marlow and Pangbourne that provided the background for the water parties of Ratty and Mole in *The Wind in the Willows* (1907).

HEAVISIDE (George) Member of the Royal Canoe Club who was inspired by MacGregor to explore the rivers Leam, Avon, Severn and Wye. The account of his voyages was published by the *Coventry Times* in 1871. In 1874 he and J. Edwin Bennett claimed to be the first canoeists to venture on the Fulda, Schwalm, Werra, Weser and Geeste (see *Canoe Cruise in Central and Northern Germany*, 1875).

HOLDING (T. H., born 1844) was a teetotal tailor who lived at Sunderland. He was an originator of the Cyclists Touring Club (C.T.C.) and the Camping Club. His publications included *Coats: how to cut and try them on* (1885), *Cutting for Stout Men* (1892) and *Cycle and Camp* (1898)—the latter was dedicated to John Mac-Gregor. He was also a keen canoeist who described his cruises in the *Cruise of the Osprey Canoe and Camp Life in Scotland* (1878) and *Watery Wanderings—mid Western Lochs* (1886). He gave his reasons for publishing his 'meagre chronicle of a commonplace cruise' as a way of promoting the 'cheapest, oldest and most rational of all aquatic sports' and that Scotland was one of the finest fields for canoe exploration in Europe. His *Camper's Handbook* (1908) included special contributions from Lady Arthur Grosvenor and Matthew Arnold.

HUGHES (Rev Robert Edgar) was a yachtsman, and his *Two Cruises with the Baltic Fleet in 1854-5* or *The Log of the 'Pet', 8 tons RTYC* (1856) is interesting for the chapter on inland navigation. After sailing a cutter yacht from Lowestoft across the North Sea to the mouth of the Eider, they arrived at Tonning and then sailed to Rendsburg, 70 miles away, with a pilot who ran the yacht hard and fast upon the mud. The *Pet* then went by canal to the Baltic Sea and Kiel, where the locals were much surprised to see so small a craft arrive from across the sea.

INWARDS (James) John MacGregor wrote in his diary that while rowing at Kew with his friend J. Inwards in the summer of 1866 he 'formed the idea of a canoe club'. Inwards was elected secretary when the club was founded in July 1866. In August 1868 he made a tour of the Highlands in a cedar sailing canoe built by Messenger of Teddington. In the course of his voyage from Inverness to the Western Coast, he sought shelter from a storm in a cave some hundred feet above Loch Ness. Here he was unexpectedly awoken in the middle of the night by an old woman for whom he made coffee. He lived at Canoe Cottage, Queens Road, Erith. (see *Cruise of the Ringleader*, 1870.)

LAWRENCE (Thomas Edward, 1889-1935), 'Lawrence of Arabia'. While a schoolboy at Oxford, he adventurously explored an underground stream by canoe from near the gasworks to the backyard of Salter's boatyard near Folly Bridge. (see, Edward Robinson, *Lawrence*, 1935.)

LESLIE (George D., 1835-1921) the artist and author described his life on the Thames in *Our River* (1881), and how in 1849 he and his brother spent many happy days rowing on the river.

LOWNDES (George) Ardent camping enthusiast who, in *Camping Sketches* (1892), recounted in a chapter entitled 'An Unnavigable River' how he and a friend one August in the 1880s rowed an outrigged dinghy down the Dorsetshire Stour from Fifehead Magdalen to Christchurch. The *Cruising Club Journal* praised the 'elegance, humour and vivacity' of his account. Indeed, there are some charming descriptive passages reflecting the joys of boating, viz: 'The river is lovely beyond description;

now running deep and still under overhanging alders, in and out of which the king-fishers flit like streaks of blue light; now walled in with flags; now bordered with arrowhead and flowering rush wherein the moorhens disport themselves and the water-rat seeks his midday meal. Here a backwater is strewn with white lilies and dark shining leaves. Here a copse comes down to the water's edge and a startled rabbit scuttles away through the long rank grass. On, on, we glide, through pleasant fields and shady groves, now hurrying beneath the huge span and unsightly ironwork of the railway, and now scraping gently against the grey stone arch of a village bridge, with a ruined castle hard by, well-known to chroniclers of old as the scene of many a revel and many a tragedy. And ever and anon the sound of troubled waters is borne upon our ears, and the moss-worn roof of a rustic mill [Fiddleford] comes into view, nestling under the shadow of lofty elms, with a white cottage or two above. The miller in his dusty coat comes out, and the miller's man comes out in no coat at all, and they stand leaning on the rickety bridge over the hatches with a little cluster of children round them, watching us as we transport our household goods down the steep bank to the pool below.' Author of *Gipsy Tents & How to Use Them* (1890).

MACDONNELL (Arthur, 1854–1930) was a distinguished scholar and linguist who in 1886 travelled by canoe to Vienna to attend the International Congress of Orient-alists, and later wrote about his experiences in *Camping Voyages on German Rivers* (1890) and also in *Camping Out* (1892) in the All-England series.

MAXWELL (Donald, 1877–1936) artist and author who was best known for his naval and travel sketches for the *Graphic*. He was also official artist to the Admiralty and for the Imperial War Museum. His yachting and motorboating experiences were published in the *Log of the Griffin* (1905), the story of a cruise from the Alps to the Thames, and *A Cruise Across Europe* (1907). In the latter he cruised from Holland to the Black Sea via King Ludwig's Canal, although arrested both in Holland and Hungary. In 1913 he wrote an account of exploring the upper Medway by motorboat.

MERSEY CANOE CLUB published an account of *Cruises on some of the Western Lochs of Scotland* by five of its members in 1884.

MILLET (F. D.) accompanied by Poulteney Bigelow (q.v.) and Alfred Parsons met together at Donaueschingen with their canoes in June 1891 and claimed that no American cruising canoe had been seen there before. For reasons not stated they parted company from Bigelow beyond Grein and reached the Black Sea on their own (see *The Danube from the Black Forest to the Black Sea*, 1893).

NOCKS (D. W.) A canal pleasure boat pioneer who was one-time mayor of Green-wich. In 1891 he presented a 'New and Original Dioramic Entertainment' at the Crystal Palace entitled 'England bisected by steam launch'. This slide presentation illustrated the voyage of the steamboat *Lizzie* from the Thames at Brentford via the

Grand Union, Stratford Canal, Worcester & Birmingham, the Severn down to Avon-mouth and back through the Kennet & Avon Canal back to the Thames. Hugh McKnight relates how these photographs were projected through the 'Nockescope', a unique gas-powered magic lantern. This had four brass-mounted lenses which enabled four slides to be project simultaneously. His machine and his programme were demonstrated to a large audience of Inland Waterways Association members at the old Lyric Theatre in Hammersmith in 1962.

PENNELL (Joseph, 1860–1926) American book illustrator and artist who illustrated with P. G. Hamerton *The Saone, A Summer Voyage*, and who together with his wife Elizabeth (1855–1936) wrote and illustrated *The Stream of Pleasure* (1891), a narrative of a journey on the Thames from Oxford to Teddington in a pair-oared skiff. The trip undertaken in August 1890 gives a good picture of the popularity of pleasure boating on the middle reaches of the Thames (see *The Adventures of an Illustrator*, Boston 1925).

70. Joseph and Elizabeth Pennell leave Oxford, 1890, on their Thames excursion

POWELL (James) a member of the London Rowing Club at Putney wrote an inter-esting account of an autumn boating trip in 1878 on the Weser, with co-author Harry Tomlinson, in a white pine pair-oared skiff built by Searle's. The pair rowed some 200 miles from Bremen to Munden via Hamelin. The following year he, with three companions (Little Buttercup, Dick Deadeye and Cousin Hebe) rowed in turns from Bordeaux to Paris. Both accounts initially appeared in *The Field*. (See *Camp Life on the Weser*, 1879; *Our Boating Trip from Bordeaux to Paris*, 1880.)

ROWLAND (H. C., 1874–1933) an American living in Paris who in a London-built motorboat, the *Beaver*, voyaged nearly 7000 miles by way of the Seine, Rhine, Danube and the Black Sea where the boat was wrecked. (See *Across Europe in a Motor Boat*, 1908.)

SUFFLING (Ernest R.) author who wrote *The Land of the Broads* (1885), in which he described the principal navigable portions of the rivers Bure, Waveney and Yare. The second edition (1887) was illustrated and enlarged to embrace 50 more miles of rivers. Later works included *A Cruise on the Friesland Meres* (1894) and *Afloat in a Gipsy Van or Adventures in the North Sea* (1895).

TAUNT (Henry, 1842–1922) Oxford photographer who compiled the first photographically illustrated guide book—*A New Map of the River Thames* (1872). The

71. Henry Taunt's houseboat, 1886

third and later editions included most of the Thames tributaries and adjoining waterways. Taunt's first trip, from Oxford to Cricklade, took place over Christmas 1860. He often voyaged with two companions in a tented 22-foot gig, some of his excursions lasting many weeks, but in the mid-1880s he favoured a houseboat 'which allowed him to work in all weathers'.

THURSTON (E. Temple, 1879–*c*. 1950) voyaged by narrow boat through the rivers and canals of the English Midlands including the Thames & Severn Canal in the first decade of the 20th century (see *The Flower of Gloster*, 1911).

WARING (Colonel George E.) An American who in the 1870s with his second wife Virginia, made a 200-mile trip in a Mosel rowboat from Metz to Coblenz, where the boat was abandoned. 'I dislike to advertise my own wares, but I am still open to offer of 10 dollars for a capital row-boat that is chained to the pier at Coblenz— first pier below the Bridge of Boats. N.B. The purchaser to pay costs.' (See *The Bride of the Rhine*, 1878.)

TOMALIN (H. E.) author of *Three Vagabonds in Friesland with a Yacht and a Camera*, published in 1907. The voyage took place in June 1906 and Arthur Marshall took the photographs.

WARREN (E. P.), with companion and co-author Cheverley (C. F. M.) and two friends, took an inrigged pair oar up the Meuse from Liège to Mezières in August 1884. At this point some of the crew jibbed at the 27 locks on the Ardennes and Aisne Canals and they took train to Soissons whence they rowed downstream on the Aisne and the Seine to Rouen. Attractive frontispiece, title page and illustrations enliven an untoward text. (See *The Wandering of the Beetle*, 1885.)

72. George Westall's motorboat *Halcyon Days*, 1908 (see page 128)

WESTALL (George), the author of *Rateable Machinery*, spent the best part of 30 summer vacations (1877–1907) cruising inland waters in motor launch, canoe and rowboat. His *Inland Cruising on the Rivers & Canals of England & Wales* (1908) included an account of a tour in 1907 by 25-foot motorboat from Brentford to Yorkshire via the Grand Junction Canal, and back via the Oxford Canal and the Thames.

BLUNT (Reginald), who with his artist brother Timothy was the first to do in England what Hamerton had done in France (see Chapter XII).* They hired a horse-drawn iron narrow-boat, the *Ada*, in which with the help of a crew of three, they cruised for three weeks in August 1887 from the Thames at Reading through the Kennet & Avon and the Wilts & Berks Canals to Abingdon. The crew slept ashore but a tent cabin was erected in the hold where 'we put a couple of folding camp-beds, a handy table, two or three camp-stools and the cases containing our cooking utensils and stores. A goodly row of hooks screwed into the gunwale and a broad plank shelf fixed across the cabin bulkhead, just below the communication window, gave places for most of the requirements of the moderately-civilised existence we contemplated'. It proved a delightful leisurely voyage. 'The charm of our progress lay in the fact that no one day was like another; and its rule was the absence of all hard-and-fast rule or plan. If we liked a place, we stopped there, and stopped as long as we liked; if we didn't, we went on. At Bradford-on-Avon, to which, in our ignorance of its unknown delights, we had allotted only a luncheon hour, we stayed three days; other places where we might well have been tempted to linger—such as Bowood or Dauntsey (near Malmesbury), we were content to glide idly by.'

The illustrated account of their voyage entitled *On Tow* was published in the *Pall Mall Magazine* and reprinted in the *Inland Waterways Association Bulletin* in October 1966.

de SALIS (Henry Rodolph), a director of canal traders Fellows, Morton & Clayton Ltd., who cruised 14,000 miles by inland waterway in the 1890s, compiling statistics and gathering information for Bradshaw's *Canals and Navigable Rivers of England and Wales* (1904).

THOMPSON (Alfred,   –1895), amateur painter, draughtsman and caricaturist. He was one of the crew of the *Water Lily on the Danube* (1852) which he illustrated. He became a cavalry officer and later studied art in Paris before becoming manager of the Theatre Royal Manchester.

---

* Occasionally commercial barges were fitted with bench seats and hired out for a church of Sunday school day outing, but rarely for a private cruise.

Chapter XV

ACCOMMODATION, CUISINE AND GUIDE BOOKS

*Lack of information about waterways—the problem of food and lodging—canoeing and camping out—cooking apparatus—guide books—*The Oarsman's Guide to the Thames *(1855)* —The Rowing Almanack and Oarsman's Companion—*H. W. Taunt's* Illustrated Map of the Thames *(1872)—Salter Brothers (1884)—Prothero and Clark (1896)—practical handbooks.*

THE DESIRE to inform others of new delights has been popular with our fellow travellers since Marco Polo brought back tales of the East. Indeed, nowadays it is difficult to find even the smallest river about which a canoe club or waterways association has not published a detailed description of the scenery, degrees of hazard, availability of boats to hire, places to avoid, eat and stay, etc. Guide books may be essential for planning, useful as aide-memoires to places to see, but then as often as not they are best cast aside. Usually they herald the disappearance of the adventurer and the arrival of the tourist.

The mid-Victorian oarsman found little information to assist him in planning his trip. Large-scale maps often lacked accurate important details and were hard to find. Baedeker or Murray handbooks were usually only helpful when the navigator had arrived at his destination. Few were aware of, or interested in studying, the factual details contained in the reference works of Priestley or Bradshaw. Beyond that, little or nothing was known about the waterways which they were intending to traverse.

In the early days of rowing and canoeing expeditions much thought was given to how best to eat and sleep. Along the main arteries of commerce, like the Rhine and the Danube, accommodation provided few nasty shocks although Mansfield, while praising Mr Bauer, an innkeeper at Linz as being 'most polite, agreeable and accommodating', added 'though, he may charge a trifle extra for these accomplishments in his account'. Boating along the smaller rivers and canals, however, posed problems. The crew of the *Undine* spent several miserable nights in overcrowded inns, suffering damp beds, mosquitoes and often sharing the one and only bedroom with bargees and other wayfarers. MacGregor, on his first two voyages, took or begged accommodation where he could, much of it of the most primitive kind. His first night in Norway was spent on a pile of straw and a flea-ridden sheepskin. For meals 'usually I got well enough fed at some village or at least a house'. Certainly, on his first voyage there were occasions when arms were weary and the sun was low and there was no way of knowing where a meal and a bed for the night was to be found. For the Baltic voyage, however, MacGregor added provisions and a cooking apparatus to the store. Indeed, on more than one occasion MacGregor had to knock up a farmer to beg for a night's lodging. After much thought and consideration as to

73. The crew of the *Undine* find accommodation for the night, 1853

whether a light tent is not better than the boat to sleep in, the *Rob Roy* for the
Near East cruise was designed to allow the occupant to sleep on board.

Hamerton, too, was prepared to lodge in the poorest country inn or cottage
(when exploring the Arroux he shared a room with a farmer's boy on the first night,
a wheelwright on the second and a poor miller's family on the third), but he found
it annoying to have to leave his etchings unfinished in order to seek a bed for the
night, with the result that much work was left incomplete or not begun because of
unfavourable weather. Hamerton's solution was to build a boat which consisted of
a wooden punt inside which was a second punt of tin. 'The metal punt was divided
into compartments in the largest of which sat the canoeist. Two had lids—one for
provisions, the other for clothing. That for provisions contained eight boxes care-
fully fitted to each other, in which were kept the different requisites for a week's
voyage, and a complete cooking apparatus. That for clothing contained a change of
dry clothes, a hammock, etc., and bedding. When night came the boat was drawn
up on the shore, and the tin punt removed from the interior of the wooden one.
Two light frames were then fixed upright in the wooden punt, and the tin one easily
lifted upon these frames. A double curtain was then fixed all round, and they had a
hut with a wooden floor, a metallic roof and canvas sides. In this hut the hammock
was easily suspended.'69 Much depended on the nature of the trip. MacGregor,
Hamerton and Baden-Powell on their exploratory voyages trusted to good fortune.
If there was no bed to be found, they slept in a barn or in their canoes. Even in

England, finding a room by a waterway was not always easy. The three canoeists who paddled from Manchester to London in 1868 generally had to sleep three to a bed. However, Dashwood and his wife were usually lucky in finding excellent food and accommodation as they sailed through Surrey and Sussex.

The crew of the *Marie* in 1873 found many good French hotels and inns, dined well and generally had a picnic lunch resting on their oars. The *Aigle d'Or* at Caudebec was 'comfort itself and cleanliness—sanded floors and a kitchen that gave you an appetite every time you passed through' and there was a delightful little inn at Poissey. Some of the hotels on the Seine were, however, disgracefully dear, but all the Loire

hotels were comfortable and good. 'Hotel homely and comfortable as one could wish, and a very pretty landlady, who popped down ducks and partridges the moment we entered. Came across some excellent wine called Beaugency', ran one entry.

Moens and his wife naturally slept in their comfortable yacht, but now and again they stayed at one of the grand hotels. Stevenson and Sir Walter Simpson were not so fortunate, and lodged where they could with mixed results, since R.L.S.'s unkempt appearance and unorthodox clothes held against him when it came to obtaining lodgings. *An Inland Voyage* is full of references to their accommodation problems. The *Hotel de la Navigation* was the worst feature of Boom, boasting dismal parlours with sanded floors, an empty birdcage and food of a nondescript character. Maubeuge had a very good inn, *Le Grand Cerf*, but at Pont sur Sambre, where the landlords and tavern keepers took them to be pedlars, they were fortunate to secure a twin-bedded room in the loft,

74. John MacGregor requests shelter, 1865 —

75. —and awakens from his bed of straw

furnished with three hat pegs and a table. There was not so much as a glass of water,
and in the morning they found two pails of water behind the street door for their
ablutions. At Landrecies the pair found better accommodation with 'real water jugs'
and plenty of furniture, and at the *Golden Sheep* in Moy they found excellent entertainment, and partridge and cabbage well above expectation; however, at La Fère
the landlady took one look at their bedraggled appearance and their limp india-
rubber bags and told them to find beds in the suburbs. 'We are too busy for the
like of you.' Fortunately they found Monsieur Bazin's friendly inn and spent an
agreeable evening in 'pleasant talk'. But at Precy they suffered 'the worst inn in
France with worse fare than even in Scotland'.

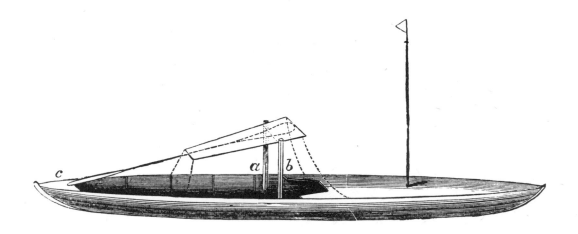

76. & 77. The *Rob Roy* canoe cabin, 1868

78. Hamerton seeking shelter, 1866 —

It was not until the 1870s that the tent became so fashioned that it could be stowed in a small boat or canoe, and once this had been achieved the practice was enthusiastically expounded by T. H. Holding, author of the *Cruise of the Osprey Canoe and Camp Life in Scotland* (1878) and James Powell, author of *Camp Life on the Weser* (1879).

'Tiphys', in his book on *Practical Canoeing*, commented that canoeing was less practised now (1883) than formerly because 'the novelty has worn off'. He went on to mention that the improvements introduced by enthusiasts had discouraged the old hand left behind by the march of events, while outsiders were deterred from taking a hand in the game by the difficulties which had been introduced. The extraordinary skill of some few canoeists and the no less marvellous complexity of the rigs in which they indulged, with impunity, through their skill, had led most people to suppose that 'canoeing except in its most elementary form of paddling was something quite beyond the powers of ordinary human beings'.

There is, however, little other evidence of this waning popularity of canoeing. 'Tiphys' himself writes: 'Even so on the Thames in summer you meet a canoe with some kind of sail every few miles'.

The worth of primitive cooking apparatus varied. MacGregor apparently had little difficulty with his cooking apparatus on his tour of the Baltic, and Baden-Powell (1871) found the Rob Roy cuisine a 'little wonder when it puts the best of its three legs forward and when its buoyant spirits fume forth in firy fury'; it could boil a quart of soup in five minutes but could only cook one item at a time and did not like wind. It was wind that defeated Stevenson and Simpson when they attempted to cook an egg with the Etna. For riverside chefs, Jerome K Jerome outlined the advantages of the methylated spirit stove over the paraffin model.

79. —and asleep in his canoe

'You get methylated pie and methylated cake. But methylated spirit is more whole-some when taken into the system in large quantities than paraffin oil.'[70]

The earliest topographical guide books to pleasure boating date from the 1850s. *The Oarsman's Guide to the Thames* informed the aquatic public about what to expect between London and Oxford; a second edition published in 1857 added information on how trips up the Thames tributaries to Bath, Basingstoke and Little-hampton might be achieved. This tiny guide (less than three inches square) gave details of all the places on the river, the locks and tolls; it tendered advice on such matters as accommodation, tackle, lock-keepers and the opening of locks. Inns and public houses providing beds were listed briefly between Lechlade and Sheerness, being those most convenient to the rower and closest to the river. At Oxford, for instance, the voyager was informed that beds were available at the *Wheatsheaf* and *Anchor Inn* in St Aldates.

The Rowing Almanack and Oarsman's Companion first appeared in 1861. This annual guide was principally concerned with racing and regattas; indeed, the preface to the first issue gave its aim as the listing of every gentleman or waterman who had taken part in any of the 200 or so matches reported. However, it did report certain feats of endurance, e.g., in 1828 Cootes completed 1000 miles rowing in 1000 hours on Chelsea Reach and a concert had been given for his benefit at the *Magpie & Stump*; also that in 1857 Messrs Balfour, Stratten and four friends had rowed 1000 miles in a four-oar gig over the rivers of France and Belgium.

The appearance of H. W. Taunt's *Map of the Thames* in 1872 saw the first guide book to be illustrated with photographs. Taunt was an ardent boating enthusiast as well as a noted photographer, and his guide to the Thames consisted of double-page coloured maps of the river on a scale of half a mile to the inch, on which were stuck

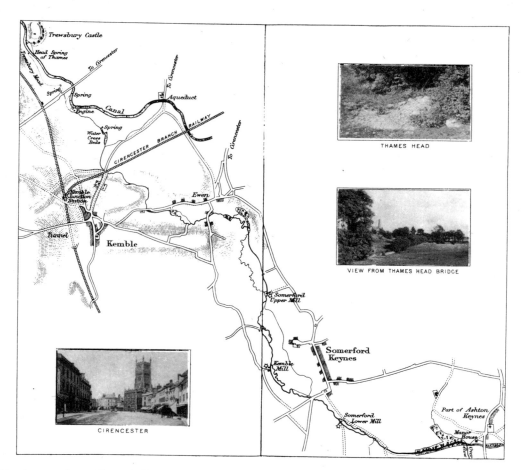

THAMES HEAD

VIEW FROM THAMES HEAD BRIDGE

CIRENCESTER

80. A page from Taunt's *New Map of the River Thames*—the first guide book to be illustrated
with photographs

three or four miniature photographs of views of the river. In between the maps
appeared the text, and at the back were found some 20 pages of advertisements for
hotels and boating establishments. The oblong first edition was quickly sold out, and
a second edition appeared the following year. The third edition, this time in octavo
size, appeared in 1878, the text being extended to include descriptions of a dozen
adjoining waterways. Further editions appeared in 1881, 1887 and 1896; a seventh
edition was advertised, but I have yet to trace a copy.

Advertisements in Taunt's guide reveal that Moss of Waterman's Cottage, Caver-
sham Bridge, let boats and 'provided good accommodation for boating, fishing and
pleasure parties; also gingerbeer, lemonade and soda water'. Tagg's of East Moulsey
supplied picnic hampers. The *Moulsey Island Hotel* could boast of 'A first class new

billiard table erected in the ornamental temple on the island'. The *Anglers' Hotel* at Teddington, conducted by the Misses Kemp, daughters of the late proprietor, Samuel Kemp, offered 'well-aired' beds and emphasized that they had no connection with the beer-shop kept by William Kemp

During the 1870s and 1880s numerous boat, canoe and punt builders and hirers were established along the Thames from Hammersmith to Oxford. Many, like Searle's, have vanished but others, like Turk of Kingston and Salter's of Oxford, still flourish. Riverside inns and hotels adapted themselves to this new type of traffic and did a roaring business welcoming water parties; some offered foreign wines and spirits of the best quality; others the finest cordials. Many offered quoits grounds, croquet lawns, bowling greens and tennis courts; the *King's Arms* at Cookham could even provide archery, shooting and football, as well as keeping horses, carriages and cows for the convenience of visitors.

Oxford boat builders, Salter Brothers, produced the first of what used to be annual guides (the 51st edition appeared in 1954) of the Thames in 1884. Advertisements in the 1880s refer to Oxford hotels like the *Mitre* being 'especially frequented by boating parties during the summer months' and as being 'one of the most economical hotels in the Kingdom'; the *Roebuck*, under the proprietorship of J. Austin Drayton, was most convenient for families, boating parties and commercial gentlemen, while the *George* claimed its suitability for boating parties, visitors or excursionists. Only the *Randolph* ignored mention of the pleasure boater and concentrated on promoting its 'excellent wines imported direct from abroad'.

The publication of Prothero & Clark's *Guide to the Rivers and Canals of Great Britain and Ireland* in 1896 marks the first comprehensive work for the oarsman. This listed over 140 waterways, but excluded rivers or canals passing through 'a grimy manufacturing district' or devoid of scenic or architectural interest. In 1904 Bradshaw's factual work of reference to canals and navigations was issued. George Westall's *Guide to Inland Cruising* appeared in 1908, and eight years later P. Bonthron's *My Holidays on Inland Waterways*, which was well reviewed in more than 85 publications.

Besides the guides on where to go, there were handbooks devoted to how best to accomplish it. The early explorers had each narrated the merits and disadvantages of their own craft, and although *A Companion to the Oarsman's Guide* (1857) gave 32 pages of helpful advice, and Routledge included *Rowing* and *Sailing* in a series of sixpenny pocket books in 1863, it was not until the 1880s that handbooks appeared on how to assess the merits of various types of craft for holiday adventure. Some, like 'Tiphys' (1883) and Hayward (1893), concentrated on canoeing; others, like Maclean & Grenfell (1898) and Crossley (1899), discussed the merits of various types of pleasure boat. Both Christopher Davies (1880) and E. F. Knight (1895) advised on small boat sailing and, with the appearance of the Badminton Library volume on *Boating* (1887), there was no lack of information on how to pursue this popular pastime.

SEARLE & SONS,

BOAT BUILDERS

TO

HER MAJESTY,

H.R.H. THE PRINCE OF WALES,

AND THE

LATE EMPEROR OF THE FRENCH,

STANGATE, LAMBETH, LONDON, S.E.

81. Searle & Sons advertisement, 1878. Searle's moved their premises to Henley-on-Thames towards the turn of the century, by which time the King of Spain, Alfonso XII, and the Sultan of Turkey had also granted them appointments

The only Prize Medal for Construction of Boats at the International
Inventions Exhibition, 1885.

BY
APPOINTMENT.

ESTABLISHED
OVER 100 YEARS.

R. J. TURK,
BOAT, PUNT, & CANOE BUILDER,
KINGSTON-ON-THAMES, SURREY.

Boats and Canoes of every kind built with all the Latest Improvements.

GENTLEMEN'S BOATS HOUSED AND REPAIRED.

HEAD QUARTERS OF THE ROYAL CANOE CLUB.

Gold Medal,

Paris, 1885.

——

Silver and

Bronze Medals

Falmouth,

1885.

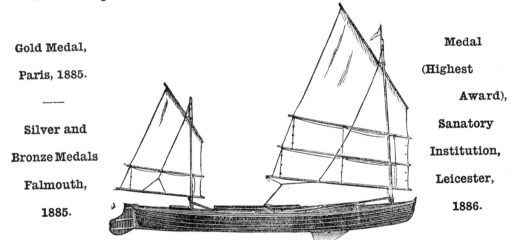

Medal

(Highest

Award),

Sanatory

Institution,

Leicester,

1886.

CRUISING CANOE, WITH SELF-REEFING GEAR SAILS.

DOUBLE-SCULLING THAMES SKIFF.

RADIX PATENT

——

Gold Medal, 1884 and 1885,
New Orleans.

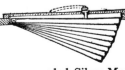

FOLDING CENTRE-BOARD,

——

Silver Medal,
Philadelphia.

Builder of the Nautilus Sailing Canoe, awarded Silver Medal, Inventions 1885 ; also builder of
Nautilus Canoe 1886 (winner of the Champion Challenge Cup), and Pearl, 1885 and 1886.

82. R. J. Turk advertisement, 1887

Fourth Edition, revised and enlarged, One Shilling.

SALTER'S GUIDE

TO THE

River Thames,

THE

RIVERS AVON, SEVERN, WYE, TRENT, AND OUSE, AND PRINCIPAL CANALS.

FOLLY BRIDGE, OXFORD.

Oxford:

ALDEN & CO., 35, CORN-MARKET STREET,

Office of "Alden's Oxford Guide."

SALTER BROS., UNIVERSITY BOAT HOUSE.

LONDON : SIMPKIN, MARSHALL, HAMILTON. KENT. AND CO., LTD.

83.   Title page to Salter's *Guide to the Thames*, 1891. The first edition was published in 1884, the 56th edition in 1959

TENTS

AND

CAMP

EQUIPMENT.

PIGGOTT BROS. & Co.

Book of Sports,

POST FREE, ON

CAMPING,
SPORTING,
SHOOTING,
FISHING,
ATHLETICS,
BOXING,
FENCING,
CRICKET, &c.

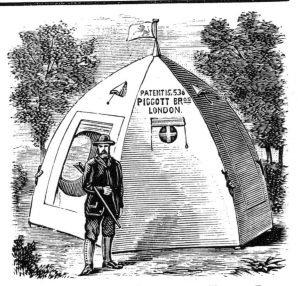

57 to 59, Bishopsgate Without, London.

Canteens,

Lanterns,

Oilskins,

&c., &c.

84. Advertisement for camping equipment, 1892

BIBLIOGRAPHY

I — Accounts of Voyages on waterways in the British Isles undertaken before 1914

1641 Taylor, John, *John Taylor's last voyage, and adventure, performed from the twentieth of July last 1641 to the tenth of September following. In which time he past, with a scullers boate from the Citie of London on to the cities and townes of Oxford, Gloucester, Shrewsbury, Bristoll, Bathe, Monmouth and Hereford . . .*

1831 Peacock, Thomas Love, *Crotchet Castle* (fiction but contemporary canal descriptions).

1861 'Bumps', *A Trip through the Caledonian Canal and Tour of the Highlands.* (Privately printed.)

1868 Dashwood, J. B., *The Thames to the Solent by Canal and Sea or the Log of the Una boat 'Caprice'* (reprinted by Shepperton Swan 1980).

1869 Anon., *The Waterway to London as explored in the 'Wanderer' and 'Ranger' with Sail, Paddle and Oar in a voyage on the Mersey, Perry, Severn and Thames and Several Canals.*

1870 Inwards, James, *Cruise of the 'Ringleader'.*

1871 Heaviside, George, *Canoe Cruise down the Leam, Avon, Severn and Wye.*

1873 'Red Rover', *Canal and River; a Canoe Cruise from Leicestershire to Greenhithe.*

1876 Davies, G. Christopher, *The 'Swan' and Her Crew or the adventures of three young naturalists and sportsmen on the Broads and Rivers of Norfolk* (7th edition 1892).

1878 Holding, T. H., *Cruise of the 'Osprey' Canoe and Camp Life in Scotland.*

1879 Kingston, W. H. G., *A yacht voyage round England* (Caledonian Canal).

1883 Davies, G. Christopher, *Norfolk Broads and Rivers or the Waterways, Lagoons and Decoys of East Anglia.*

1883 Speed, H. Fiennes, *Cruises on Small Yachts and Big Canoes* (reprinted with *More Cruises* by Maude Speed, 1926).

1886 Holding, T. H., *Watery Wanderings mid Western Lochs.*

1887 Clarke, J. F. M., *Three Weeks in Norfolk, being a portion of the 'Rover's' Log.*

1888 Black, William, *The Strange Adventures of a Houseboat* (fiction but contemporary canal descriptions).

1889 Jerome, Jerome K., *Three Men in a Boat.*

1889 Doughty, H. M., *Summer in Broadland: Gipsying in East Anglian Waters.*

1891 Cotes, V. C., *Two Girls on a Barge.*

1891   Pennell, Joseph and Elizabeth, *The Stream of Pleasure, a narrative of a journey on the Thames from Oxford to London.*

1892   Laffan, Mrs. R. S. de Courcy, *The Cruise of the 'Tomahawk'.*

1892   Lowndes, G. R., *Camping Sketches* (chapter on the Dorsetshire Stour).

1893   Emerson, P. H., *On English Lagoons being an account of the Voyage of two amateur wherrymen on the Norfolk and Suffolk Rivers and Broads.*

1895   'Bickerdyke, John' (C. H. Cook), *The Best Cruise on the Broads.*

1895   Laing, C. C., *A week on the Bure, Ant and Thurne.*

1896   Dodd, A. B., *On the Broads.*

1899   Anon., *Chester–Kendal Canal Trip.*

1911   Ledger, W. E., *The 'Blue Bird' among the Norfolk reeds with some reflections on the water.*

1911   Temple Thurston, E., *The Flower of Gloster* (reprinted 1913, and 1968 with introduction by L. T. C. Rolt).

1912   Finch, R. J., *To the West of England by Canal.*

1916   Aubertin, C. J., *A Caravan Afloat* (reprinted by Shepperton Swan 1981).

1916   Bonthron, P., *My Holidays on Inland Waterways* (3rd edition 1919), period 1890–1915.

1920   Barnes, Eleanor (later Lady Yarrow), *As the Water Flows.*

1920   Patterson, A. H., *Through Broadland in a Breydon punt.*

1921   Farrar, C. F., *Ouse's Silent Tide.*

1921   Neal, Austin, E., *Canals, Cruises and Contentment.*

1933   Bliss, William, *Through the Heart of England by Waterway.*

1977   Farrant, A., *Rowing Holiday by Canal in 1873.*

II – Accounts of Voyages published in English and undertaken on Waterways in Europe and the Near East before 1914

1852   Mansfield, R. B., *The Log of the 'Water Lily'*—account of a voyage on the Neckar, Maine, Moselle and Rhine.

1853   Mansfield, R. B., *The 'Water Lily' on the Danube*—being a brief account of the perils of a pair-oar during a voyage from Lambeth to Pesth (Budapest).

1854   Harvey, E. G., *Our Cruise in the 'Undine'. The Journal of An English Pair-Oar Expedition through France, Baden, Rhenish Bavaria, Prussia and Belgium by The Captain.*

1854   Mansfield, R. B., *The Log of the 'Water Lily' during two cruises on the Rhine, Main, Moselle and Danube (1851–2)* (the fifth edition in 1873 included the voyage on the Saone and Rhône in 1854).

1866   MacGregor, John, *A Thousand Miles in the 'Rob Roy' Canoe on rivers and lakes of Europe* (21st edition 1908).

1867   Hamerton, P. G., *A Canoe Voyage.*

1867   MacGregor, John, *The 'Rob Roy' on the Baltic* (10th edition 1894).

1868   MacGregor, John, *The Voyage Alone in the Yawl 'Rob Roy'* (7th edition *c.* 1905, reprinted 1954 with introduction by Arthur Ransome).

1868 Gordon, Hon. James, *A Canoe Voyage in the 'Pothion'*.
1869 MacGregor, John, *The 'Rob Roy' on the Jordan, Nile, Red Sea and Gennesareth etc.* (8th (actually 10th) edition 1904).
1871 Hamerton, P. G., *The Unknown River* (the Arroux) (reprinted 1874).
1871 Baden-Powell, W., *Canoe Travelling: log of a cruise on the Baltic*.
1874 Molloy, J. C., *Our Autumn Holiday on French Rivers* (reprinted 1879).
1875 Heaviside, George & Bennett, J. E., *Canoe Cruise in Central and North Germany on the Fulda, Schwalm, Werra, Weser and Geeste in 1874*.
1876 Robinson, C. E. N., *The Cruise of the 'Widgeon'*.
1876 Moens, W. J. C., *Through France and Belgium by river and canal in the steam yacht 'Ytene'*.
1878 Stevenson, R. L., *An Inland Voyage* (10th edition 1899, illustrated by Noel Rooke, 1908).
1878 Waring, G. E., *The Bride of the Rhine. Two hundred miles in a Mosel row-boat*.
1879 Powell, James & Tomlinson, H., *Camp Life on the Weser*.
1880 Powell, James, *Our Boating Trip from Bordeaux to Paris*.
1882 [Lees, J. A. & Clutterbuck, W. J.], *Three in Norway by Two of Them* (reprinted 1883).
1885 Warren, E. P. & Cleverly, C. F. M., *The Wanderings of the 'Beetle'*.
1886 Davies, G. Christopher, *On Dutch Waterways: the Cruise of the SS 'Atlanta' on the Rivers & Canals of Holland & the North of Belgium*.
1887 Hamerton, P. G., *The Saone: a Summer Voyage*.
1889 Doughty, H. M., *Friesland Meres and through the Netherlands; the Voyage of a Family in a Norfolk Wherry*.
1889 Knight, E. F., *The 'Falcon' on the Baltic. A coasting voyage from Hammersmith to Copenhagen in a three-ton yacht*.
1890 MacDonell, A. A., *Camping Voyages on German Rivers* (period 1884–8).
1891 Brougham, Reginald, *A Cruise on Friesland 'Broads'*.
1891 Pain, R., *In a Canadian Canoe*.
1892 Bigelow, Poultney, *Paddles and Politics down the Danube*.
1892 Millet, F. D., *The Danube from the Black Forest to the Black Sea*.
1892 Doughty, H. M., *Our Wherry in Wendish Lands; from Friesland through the Mecklenburg Lakes to Bohemia*.
1893 Bird, A. F. R., *Boating in Bavaria, Austria and Bohemia, down the Danube, Moldan and Elbe*.
1894 Suffling, E. R., *A Cruise on the Friesland Meres*.
c.1895 Donner, Mrs. J. A., *Down the Danube in an Open Boat*.
1902 Koebel, A. F., *Dinghey dawdle: Danubian and other. From Thames to Black Sea*.
1905 Maxwell, Donald, *The Log of the 'Griffin'; the Story of a Cruise from the Alps to the Thames*.
1907 Maxwell, Donald, *A Cruise across Europe* (reprinted 1925).
1907 Tomalin, H. F., *Three Vagabonds in Friesland with a Yacht and a Camera*.
1908 Rowland, H. C., *Across Europe in a motor boat; a chronicle of the adventures of the motor boat 'Beaver' on a voyage of nearly seven thousand miles through

Europe by way of the Seine, the Rhine, the Danube and the Black Sea.

1910 Anderson, R. C., *Canoeing and Camping Adventures; being an account of three cruises in Northern Waters.*

1910 Pears, C., *From the Thames to the Seine.*

1910 Scott-James, R. A., *An Englishman in Ireland: impressions of a journey in a canoe by river, lough and canal.*

1913 Chatterton, E. Keble, *Through Holland in the 'Vivette', the cruise of a 4-tonner from the Solent to the Zuyder Zee through the Dutch waterways.*

1913 Thorpe, E. E., *The Seine from Havre to Paris.*

1914 Pears, C., *From the Thames to the Netherlands; a Voyage in the Waterways of Zealand and down the Belgian coast.*

1914 Bennett, Arnold, *From the Log of the 'Velsa'*, New York (UK edition 1920).

1915 Chase, Mrs Lewis, *A Vagabond Voyage through Brittany.*

III — Works of Reference and Instruction, Guide Books, etc.

1831 Priestley, J., *Historical Account of the Navigable Rivers, Canals and Railways throughout Great Britain* (reprinted 1969).

1833 *Lengths and Levels to Bradshaw's Maps of the Canals, Navigable Rivers and Railways.*

1848 Halkett, Lieut. Peter, *The Boat-Cloak, constructed of Macintosh india-rubber cloth, with paddle, umbrella-sail, bellows etc., also an inflated india-rubber-cloth-boat for two paddlers.*

c. 1855 *The Oarsman's Guide to the Thames.*

1857 *The Oarsman's Guide to the Thames and other Rivers.*

1857 *A companion to the Oarsman's Guide.*

1872 Taunt's *Illustrated Map of the Thames* (reprinted 1873, 1879, 1881, 1887, 1897; the third and later editions included adjacent river navigations and canals).

1876 MacGregor, John, *Canoe* (Encyclopaedia Britannica 9th edition).

1881 Kemp, Dixon & Davies, G. C., *Practical Boat Building and Sailing.*

1882 *The Thames Guide Book from Lechlade to Richmond for Boating Men.*

1882 Davies, G. Christopher, *The Handbook to the Rivers & Broads of Norfolk and Suffolk* (50th edition 1914).

1883 *'Tiphys' Practical Canoeing.*

1884 Salter's *Guide to the River Thames* (57th edition 1960).

1885 Suffling, E. R., *The Land of the Broads.*

1887 Woodgate, W. B., *Boating* (Badminton Library).

1889 Knight, E. F., *Sailing.*

1890 Lowndes, G. R., *Gipsy Tents and How to Use Them.*

1892 Macdonell, A. A., *Camping Out.*

1893 Hayward, J. D., *Canoeing with Sail and Paddle.*

1893 Hayward, J. D. & Macdonell, A. A., *Canoeing and Camping Out.*

1896 Prothero, F. T. E. & Clark, W. A., *A New Oarsman's Guide to the Rivers and Canals of Great Britain and Ireland.*

1897 Baden-Powell, Warington, Canoes and Canoeing (*The Encyclopaedia of Sport* vol. I).

1897 De Salis, H. R., *Chronology of Inland Navigation*.

1897 *Dicken's Dictionary of the Thames*.

1898 Maclean, D. H. & Grenfell, W. H., *Rowing, Punting and Punts*.

1899 Crossley, Sydney, *Pleasure and Leisure Boating*.

1901 Knight, E. F., *Small-Boat Sailing*.

1904 De Salis, H. R., *Bradshaw's Canals and Navigable Rivers*.

1907 Hamerton, J. A., *In the Track of Stevenson and elsewhere in old France*.

1907 Corbett, J., *The River Irwell*.

1908 Westall, George, *Inland Cruising on the Rivers and Canals of England and Wales*.

1914 Thacker, Fred S., *The Thames Highway—General History* (reprinted 1968).

1920 Thacker, Fred S., *The Thames Highway—Locks and Weirs* (reprinted 1968).

1930 Brittain, F., *Oar, Scull and Rudder: a bibliography of rowing*.

1934 Bliss, W., *Canoeing*.

1936 Luscombe, W. G., *Canoeing*.

1950 Hadfield, Charles, *British Canals*.

1965 Vine, P. A. L., *London's Lost Route to the Sea*.

1968 Vine, P. A. L., *London's Lost Route to Basingstoke*.

1969 Owen, D. E., *Water Rallies*.

1972 Vine, P. A. L., *The Royal Military Canal*.

1974 Bolland, R. R., *Victorians on the Thames*.

1975 McKnight, Hugh, *The Shell Book of Inland Waterways*.

1978 McKnight, Hugh, *The Guinness Guide to Waterways of Western Europe*.

1981 Burstall, P., *The Golden Age of the Thames*.

IV — Autobiographies, Biographies and Correspondence

Balfour, Graham, *The Life of Robert Louis Stevenson*, 2 vols., 1901.

Colvin, Sidney, *The Letters of Robert Louis Stevenson*, 2 vols., 1899.

Connolly, Joseph, *Jerome K Jerome*, 1982.

Dictionary of National Biography, entries relating to R. B. Mansfield, Edmund Harvey, Warington Baden-Powell, James Molloy, William Moens.

Farson, Negley, *The Way of a Transgressor*, 1935.

Hamerton, Philip Gilbert, *An Autobiography and a Memoir by His Wife*, 1897.

Hodder, Edwin, *John MacGregor*, 1894.

Houghton, R. E. C., Introduction and Notes to *An Inland Voyage*, 1926.

Jerome, J. K., *Autobiography*, 1926.

Mansfield, R. B., *New and Old Chips from an Old Block*, 1896.

Moss, Alfred, *Jerome K Jerome*, 1928.

Pennell, Joseph, *The Adventures of an Illustrator*, 1925.

Ransome, Arthur, *John MacGregor: Introduction to the Mariners*, library edition *The Voyage Alone in the Yawl 'Rob Roy'*, 1954.

NOTES

1. Charles Dickens, *Sketches of London*, 1835, Ch. X The River.
2. P. A. L. Vine, *London's Lost Route to the Sea*, 1965, p. 210.
3. R. B. Mansfield, *The 'Water Lily' on the Danube*, 1854, p. 255, Ch. XVIII.
4. John MacGregor, *A Thousand Miles in the 'Rob Roy' Canoe*, 1866, p. 5.
5. Warington Baden-Powell, *Canoe Travelling*, 1871, p. 1.
6. Thomas Wood, Preface to *The Oarsman's Guide to the Thames*, c. 1855.
7. R. B. Mansfield, *The 'Water Lily' on the Danube*, 1853, p.
8. [Edmund Harvey], *Our Cruise in the 'Undine'*, 1854, pp. 79–80.
9. Diary entry 10 August 1849 quoted by Edwin Hodder, *John MacGregor*, 1894, p. 64.
10. Ibid., pp. 204–5.
11. *A Thousand Miles in the 'Rob Roy' Canoe*, 1866, p. 5.
12. Ibid., p. 72.
13. Ibid., p.
14. Ibid., p. 222.
15. Ibid., pp. 22–3.
16. Edwin Hodder, *John MacGregor*, 1894, pp. 207–8.
17. *A Thousand Miles*, op. cit., pp. 8–9.
18. *'Rob Roy' on the Baltic*, 1867, p. 281.
19. *The Voyage Alone in the Yawl 'Rob Roy'*, 1868, pp. 241–2.
20. Philip Gilbert Hamerton, *An Autobiography and a Memoir by His Wife*, 1897, p. 220.
21. *The Unknown River*, 1871, p. 4.
22. Ibid., p. 45.
23. *The Oarsman's Guide to the Thames and Other Rivers*, 2nd edition 1857 by a member of the Leander Club [Thomas Wood] published by Searle & Sons, boat builders to Her Majesty, HRH The Prince of Wales and the Emperor of the French. Price 2s.
24. Anon., *The Waterway to London*, 1869, p. 13.
25. Ibid., p. 16.
26. Ibid., p. 25.
27. Ibid., p. 68.
28. Warington Baden-Powell, *Canoe Travelling: log of a cruise on the Baltic*, 1871, p. vi.
29. Ibid., p. viii.

30. William Harcourt and Olave Lady Baden-Powell, *The Two Lives of a Hero*, 1964, p. 30.
31. *The Encyclopaedia of Sport*, ed. The Earl of Suffolk and Berkshire, vol. I, 1897, p. 170.
31a. *The Log of the 'Water Lily'*, preface to fifth edition, 1873.
32. James Molloy, *Our Autumn Holiday on French Rivers*, 1874, p. 343.
33. Ibid., p. 372.
34. Ibid., p. 7.
35. Ibid., pp. 98–9.
36. Graham Balfour, *The Life of Robert Louis Stevenson*, vol. I, 1901, p. 143.
37. William Moens, *Through France and Belgium by River and Canal in the Steam Yacht 'Ytene'*, 1876, p. 71.
38. Ibid., p. 131.
39. Robert Louis Stevenson, *An Inland Voyage*, 1878, p. 74.
40. *Through France and Belgium*, op. cit., pp. 125–6.
41. Ibid., p. 152.
42. AL 30 July 1876 to Mrs Sitwell quoted by Sidney Colvin *The Letters of Robert Louis Stevenson*, 1899, vol. I, pp. 116–7.
43. AL 9 September 1876 from Compiègne quoted by Balfour, vol. I, p. 143.
44. Balfour, vol. I, p. 133.
45. R. L. Stevenson: *A Critical Study*, 1914.
46. Stevenson, *An Inland Voyage*, pp. 9–10.
47. Ibid., pp. 76–7.
48. AL undated to W. E. Henley quoted by Colvin op. cit., pp. 117–8.
49. J. A. Hammerton, *In the Track of Stevenson and elsewhere in Old France*, 1907.
50. G. F. Morton, *Hike and Track-Education in the School of Adventure*, 1928.
51. *An Inland Voyage*, op. cit., p. 47.
52. Ibid., pp. 69–70.
53. *An Inland Voyage*. Dedication to Sir Walter Grindlay Simpson.
54. AL quoted in Philip Gilbert Hamerton, op. cit., p. 490.
55. Ibid., pp. 546–7.
56. Hitherto unpublished undated AL in the author's possession probably written from Autun in September 1886.
57. P. G. Hamerton, *The Saone: A Summer Voyage*, 1887, p. 268.
58. Ibid., p. 7.
59. Philip Gilbert Hamerton, op. cit., p. 552.
60. *The Times*, 7 November 1894.
61. J. K. Jerome, *Autobiography*, 1926, p. 104.
62, J. K. Jerome, *Three Men in a Boat*, 1889, p. 56.
63. Ibid., p. 175.
64. Ibid., p. 219.
65. Ibid., p. 270.
66. Joseph Connolly, *Jerome K Jerome*, 1982, p. 77.
67. J. K. Jerome, *Three Men in a Boat*, March 1909, author's advertisement.
68. Ibid.

69. P. G. Hamerton, *The Unknown River*, 1871, p. 52. These and other details were excluded from the 1874 edition since 'my preparations were of the kind so well-known to canoe-men'.

70. *Three Men in a Boat*, op. cit., p. 28.

INDEX

BOAT BUILDERS ARE LISTED UNDER A GENERIC HEADING AS ARE CANALS, LAKES AND RIVERS